# ABSTRACT OF LAND GRANT SURVEYS 1761–1791

### [AUGUSTA & ROCKINGHAM COUNTIES, VIRGINIA]

By
PETER CLINE KAYLOR

*Assisted by*
GEORGE WARREN CHAPPELEAR

CLEARFIELD

Originally Published
Rockingham Historical Society
Harrisonburg, Virginia
1938


Reprinted
Genealogical Publishing Co., Inc.
Baltimore, 1976


Reprinted for
Clearfield Company, Inc. by
Genealogical Publishing Co., Inc.
Baltimore, Maryland
1991, 2002, 2005

Library of Congress Catalogue Card Number 76-16887
International Standard Book Number: 0-8063-0725-0

*Made in the United States of America*

# PREFACE

Realizing the importance of land conveyance records to any genealogist who may attempt to write biography and knowing that the Rockingham County deed records were partly burned in 1864, thereby effacing many deeds, the authors of this book have made an abstract and index of land surveys of Augusta and Rockingham counties from 1751 to 1791. There is recorded in these abstracts the name of the person for whom the survey was made, the location of the land, and the name of the owner or owners of the adjoining land. These surveys were made for original land patents by Thomas Lewis, surveyor for Augusta County, and later for Rockingham County, from April 23, 1751, to February 22, 1782. The entries from 1782 to 1791 were made by Alexander Herring, surveyor for Rockingham County. The assistants were John Poage, James Trrimble, Wm. Preston, Andrew Lewis, Gawn Hamilton, John Lincoln, and Ralph Lofftus.

Those persons who may desire additional names of the first settlers in Rockingham County are referred to Land Survey Books A, B, and C and to Alexander Herring's Road Precinct Book of 1820, and John Cowan Road Precinct Book for 1842, which is on file in the clerk's office of Rockingham County.

Publication of this book has ben ordered by the Board of supervisors of Rockingham County in order to preserve the records herein contained. The Rockingham Historical Society wishes to acknowledge its appreciation of the assistance given the society by the Board of Supervisors.

# Abstract of Surveys

## BOOK O-1

### Page 1

John Lewis, 104 acres between Shenandoah River and the mountain. Adjacent to Joseph Hanna. April 23, 1761.

Robert Frazer, 75 acres, corner to John Lewis. Adjacent to Joseph Hanna. April 23, 1761.

Nicholas Huffman, 85 acres, between the Shenandoah River and Peaked Mountain. October 20, 1761.

Phillip Harless, 80 acres, Givens Mill Run. Adjacent to John Givens. March 17, 1762.

James Givens, 30 acres. Givens Draft. March 17, 1769.

Samuel Bell, 40 acres, Givens Mill Run. Adjoining James Givens. March 17, 1762.

John Seller, 330 acres, Lick Run. Adjoining Henry Pirkey, Null, Kissling. May 11, 1762.

### Page 2

Ann Perkey, 190 acres, north side of Shenandoah River. Adjoining Henry Pirkey, Miller, Burk, Sellers. May 4, 1762.

Henry Sellers, 205 acres, between Shenandoah River and Peaked Mountain. Adjoining Stephen Harnsberger. May 3, 1762.

Mathias Sulcher, 85 acres, Shenandoah River and opposite the lower end of an island. Adjoining Lungs (Long). May 7, 1762.

Thomas Burk, 320 acres, Dry Run, north side of Shenandoah River. May 6, 1762.

Jacob Persinger, 130 acres between Cub Run and Stony Run. Adjoining Jacob Herman (Harman). April 27, 1762.

Jacob Man, 95 acres between Shenandoah River and Peaked Mountain. Adjoining John Hetrick (Hedrick). April 27, 1762.

Peter Miller, 250 acres, Stony Run. Adjoining Barnet Man, Herman.

### Page 3

Mathias Scarse, 130 acres between Shenandoah River and

Peaked Mountain. Mentioned Switzers Meadows. May 3, 1762.

Christopheer Kissling, 96 acres, Quails Run. Adjoining Mathias Sease. March 3, 1762.

Stephen Conrod, 24 acres, Between Lick Run and Boons Run. Adjoining John Sellers, Nulls, Wood, Kissling. May 4, 1762.

Nicholas Null, 220 acres, Lick Run and Boones Run. May 5, 1762.

Jacob Runkle, 225 acres, branch of Boons Run. May 5, 1762.

George Null, 64 acres, Lick Run. Adjoining Perkey, Nickolus Null, Ann Perkey. May 5, 1762.

Danaiel Sink, 100 acres, opposite to the mouth of Naked Creek, on the north side of the Shenandoah River. May 6, 1762.

Stephen Harnsberg (Harnsberger), 11 acres, Shenandoah River. Adjoining Fouch. May 7, 1762.

Francis Kertley, 210 acres, Elk run. Adjoining Earley, Grubb. September 29, 1762.

Page 4

Jacob Mire, 50 acres, East side Shenandoah River. Adjoining his own land. September 30, 1762.

Conrod Blows 160 acres, North side Naked Creek. Adjoining Henry Null. September 30, 1762.

Windle Evert, 300 acres, Naked Creek. Adjoining Blows. September 30, 1762.

Francis Kirtley, 220 acres, Boons Run. Adjoining Woods. October 1, 1762.

Samuel Thornhill, 70 acres, Between Stony Run and Dry Run. Adjoining Jacob Runkle. October 1, 1762.

Andrew Lewis, 1740 acres, Branch of Green Brier. Adjoining John Robinson. April 29, 1751.

Page 5

John Archer, 260 acres, Middle River. Adjoining his own land. William Anderson. December 1, 1760.

Andrew Lewis, 1200 acres, Between Indian Creek and Green River. April 16, 1751.

Andrew Lewis, 480 acres, Both sides of Green Brier River. Adjoining John Robinson. October 1, 1751.

Page 6

David Ralston, 307 acres, South fork Linvil Creek. Men-

tioned.
Abraham Hite, 1200 acres from Robert McCoy (McCay),
Josh Hite, William Duff and Robert Green. McCay,
Hite, Duff, and Green, Patentees of 7009 acres. April
22, 1761.
John Wright, 550 acres, both forks of Linvils Creek. Mentioned Abraham Hite, Robert McCoy (McCay), Jost
Hite, William Duff, and Robert Green. Adjoining Jeremiah Harrison, Michael Waring. April 22, 1761.
Jeremiah Harrison, 400 acres, Fork of Linvils Creek. Mentioned Abraham Hite, 1200 acres, Robert McCoy, Jost
Hite, William Duff, and Robert Green. Adjoining David
Ralston, John Wright. August 22, 1761.

Page 7

John Allison, 245 acres Middle River. Adjoining John Keer,
James Hamilton, his own land. February 9, 1762.
Jacob Gillespy, 215 acres, Briery Branch. Nov. 27, 1761.
Bastian Hover, 135 acres, South Branch of Potomac. Adjoining Pete Smiths. December 3, 1761.
George Bush, 65 acres, South fork of Patomack. Adjoining
his own land. Frederick Keester. December 4, 1761.
Pete Smith, 54 acres, South Branch Potomuck. Adjoining
Greens, December 2, 1761.
William and Andrew Russel, 120 acres, Draft Long Meadows. Adjoining his own land. Kenneley.
George Bush 33 acres, Potomick, Brushy Fork. Dec. 3, 1761.

Page 8

Samuel Hinds, 375 acres, Middle River. Adjoining Edward
Rutledge, Kerr, Thomas Story. May 6, 1761.
Hugh Allen, 140 acres, Middle River. Adjoining Patrick
Crawford, his own land. May 5, 1761.
Joist Hinkle, 220 acres, North fork Potomack. April 3, 1761.
Moses Elsworth, 60 acres, North Branch of Potomac. April
3, 1761.
Mark Swadley, 130 acres, Branch of Potomack. April
15, 1761.
Frederick Kester, 67 acres, Branch Potomack. Adjoining
his own land. April 14, 1761.
George Bush, 44 acres, Fork of Potomack. Adjoining his
own land.
Mark Swadley, 40 acres Branch of Potomack, Apr. 15, 1761.

## Page 9

George Poage, 37 acres, Middle River. Adjoining David Stephenson, Thomas Stephenson. March 18, 1761.

Alexander Heron, 38 acres, Linvils Creek. Adjoining David Rolston, Samuel Harrison, Hites. April 22, 1761.

George Poage, 46 acres. Middle River. Adjoining Stevenson, Hughes. March 18, 1761.

Jacob Peters, 69 acres, South Branch Potomack. Adjoining his own land. April 10, 1761.

John Francis, 400 acres, Long Glade. Adjoining his own land. John Archer. March 26, 1761.

Joseph Skedmore, 54 acres, South Branch Potomack. March 30, 1761.

John Stephenson, 54 acres, Branch of Naked Creek. Adjoining Thomas McCutchin, his own land. March 17, 1761.

David Frame, 77 acres, Draft of Naked Creek. Adjoining his own land. Robert McCutchin. March 7, 1761.

## Page 10

Mathew and William Ralston, 20 acres, Mossy Creek. Adjoining their own land. March 27, 1761.

Moses Hall, 63 acres, Mossy Creek. Adjoining his own land. William. March 26, 1761.

William Hamilton, 50 acres, Middle River. Adjoining his own land. James Blair. June 13, 1761.

James Blair, 60 acres, Long Glade. Adjoining Alexander Blair, James Blair, William Frame. June 12, 1761.

James Blair, 260 acres Branch Naked Creek. Adjoining John Blair. June 10, 1761.

Paul Shever, 200 acres, South Branch of Potomack. Adjoining Sheltons. April 6, 1761.

Martin Shobe, 130 acres, South Branch of Potomack. April 11, 1761.

Peter Smith, 110 acres, South fork of Potomack. April 14, 1761.

## Page 11

Johnathan Douglas, 323 acres, Adjoining Francis Green, James Green, Claypol. April 30, 1761.

George Coil, 67 acres, South Branch of Potomack. April 1, 1761.

Jacob Aberman, 137 acres, South fork of Potomack. Adjoining Switzer. March 30, 1761.

Abraham Smith, 142 acres South Branch of Potomack. April 6, 1761.

Daniel Pounder, 87 acres, East Draft of Cooks Creek. October 18, 1760.

James Thomas, 78 acres, Branch of North Shenandoah River. Adjoining Nalls, Borden, Shoemaker. April 30, 1761.

Daniel Harrison and Joseph Skidamore, 110 acres, north fork, South Branch of Potomack. April 9, 1761.

Page 12

Daniel Harrison and Joseph Skidmore, 64 acres, South Branch Potomack. April 8, 1761.

Daniel Harrison and Joseph Skidmore, 156 acres, South Branch Potomack. April 8, 1761.

Daniel Harrison and Joseph Skidmore, 47 acres, South Branch Potomack. April 8, 1761.

Daniel Harrison and Joseph Skidmore, 55 acres, South Branch Potomack. April 7, 1761.

Daniel Harrison and Joseph Skidmore, 62 acres, South Branch Potomack. April 2, 1761.

Daniel Harrison and Joseph Skidmore, 98 acres, South Branch Potomack. April 7, 1761.

Daniel Harrison and Joseph Skidmore, 97 acres, South Branch Potomack. April 3, 1761.

Daniel Harrison and Joseph Skidmore, 82 acres, South Branch Potomack. April 2, 1761.

Daniel Harrison and Joseph Skidmore, 49 acres, South Branch Potomack. April 7, 1761.

Daniel Harrison and Joseph Skidmore, 20 acres, South Branch Potomack. April 2, 1761.

Page 13

Joseph Davis, 110 acres, James River, Branch of Loony Creek. March 16, 1762.

James Edmenson, 116 acres, Buffilo Hill on Buffilo Creek. March 5, 1762.

Gilbert Crawford, 50 acres, Buffilo Creek. March 23, 1762.

Wallace Estill, 94 acres, James River opposite Vanderpools Gap. March 13, 1762.

Robert Shannon, 98 acres, Camp Mountains. Mar. 17, 1762.

George Gibson, 66 acres, North Mountain. Adjoining John Low. March 24, 1762.

John Low, 83 acres, Coliers Branch of Buffilo Creek. Adjoining George Gibson. March 24, 1762.
John Willey, 46 acres, Adjoining his own land. March 22, 1762.
Halbart McClure, 42 acres, House Mountain. Mar. 24, 1762.

## Page 14

Richard Bush, 234 acres, James River. Adjoining Charles Wilson, his own land. May 10, 1762.
James Logan, 180 acres, Forks of James River. May 11, 1762.
William Robinson, 94 acres, Forks James River mentioned Fees Creek. Adjoining John Gilmore. May 11, 1762.
Edward Gill, 60 acres, Forks of James River. Mentioned Camp Mountain. May 12, 1762.
Patrick Danney, 68 acres, Forks of James River. Mentioned House Mountain. March 23, 1762.
Alexander and John Walker, 210 acres, Forks of James River. Mentioned Buffilo and Broad Creeks. Adjoining Moris Ofrails. March 15, 1762.
Thomas Breets, 90 acres, Buffilo Creek. Mentioned Gibson land. March 18, 1762.
Robert Loony, 60 acres, James River. Adjoining his own land. March 17, 1762.
James (Obryan), 98 acres, Draft of Buffilo Creek. March 18, 1762.

## Page 15

John Lowny, 110 acres, North Branch James River. Adjoining John Dealy, his own land. February 5, 1762.
Arthur McClune, 62 acres, Forks James River. January 29, 1762.
John Greenlee, 140 acres, James River. Mentioned Elk Creek. Adjoining James McDowel. November 25, 1761.
James McDowel, 120 acres, James River. Mentioned Ceder Creek. November 26, 1761.
Stephen Arnold, 220 acres, James River. Mentioned Elk Creek. November 26, 1761.
John Paxton, 150 acres, North Branch James River. Adjoining Robert Youngs. December 19, 1760.
Hugh (Mare), 85 acres, Forks James River. Dec. 18, 1761.
Archebald Reaigh Jr., 24 acres, Hays Creek. Adjoining Seth Wilson, Burdon. February 20, 1762.

Page 16
John Lewis, son of Thomas Lewis and John Lewis, son of
Andrew Lewis, 580 acres, Jacksons River. Mentioned
Branch of Great Warm Springs. September 27, 1762.
In this plat is the following: "Settled with the col-
ledge for all the surveys Recorded before this."
Margaret Patterson, 196 acres, Buffeto (Buffilo) Creek a
Branch of Renark (Roanoke). Adjoining William
Grymes, William Caravans, Graham. Sept. 27, 1762.
James Lawerence, 150 acres, Cub Run. Mentioned Peaked
Mountain. December 6, 1762.
John Carpenter, 115 acres, North River above the mouth of
Naked Creek. March 3, 1762.
Samuel Lisk, 150 acres, North River of Shenandoah. Ad-
joining John Lisk. March 3, 1762.

Page 17
Alexander Heron, 88 acres, Cooks Creek. Adjoining his
own land, John Trotter, Edwards. February 25, 1762.
John Young, 53 acres, Middle River of Shenandoah. Ad-
joining Alexander Crigs, John Hall. March 22, 1763.
Benjammin Kinley, 80 acres, Brocks Creek at the foot of
the North Mountain. Mentioned Bear Wallow. April
12, 1762.
John Grattan, 140 acres, Brocks Gap. Adjoining Burden.
April 12, 1762.
Abraham Bird, 235 acres, Brocks Gap. Adjoining Conrod
Lamb. April 14, 1762.
Jacob Crambo, 100 acres, Brocks Gap. Adjoining Conrod
Lamb,and James Bagg. April 14, 1762.
John Compton, 115 acres, Lick Branch in Brocks Gap. Ad-
joining his own land. April 15, 1762.

Page 18
William Bumpass, 267 acres, Cooks Creek. Adjoining Dan-
iel Love, Mathew Blacks. April 27, 1762.
John Dunkle, 44 acres, South Branch of Potomack. Adjoin-
ing Lewdwich Waggoner. April 27, 1762.
Lewdwick Waggoner, 47 acres, South Branch Potomack.
Adjoining John Dunkle. April 27, 1762.
Jacob Hornbrier, 229 acres, South Branch Potomack. Ad-
joining Dyche. April 30, 1762.
Joseph Skidmore Jr., 150 acres, South Branch Potomack.

Adjoining George Caplinger. April 30, 1762.
Jacob Peters, 60 acres, South Fork Potomack. Adjoining
Dyche. May 1, 1762.
Joseph Skidmore and David Haneson, 80 acres, South
Branch Potomack. Mentioned Middle fork, adjoining
the Crabe Apple Bottom. May 4, 1762.
Henry Paninger, 12 acres, South Branch Potomack. May
1, 1762.

## Page 19

Andrew Erwin, 96 acres, Mossey Creek. Adjoining Davison. June 15, 1762.
James McCoy, 160 acres, Mossey Creek. Adjoining his own
land. John McCoy. June 15, 1762.
John McCoy, 80 acres, Mossey Creek. Adjoining his own
land. Ralston. May 12, 1762.
John McCarney, 66 acres, North River of Shenandoah. Ad-
joining his own land. June 17, 1762.
James Hughs, George Willson, Sampson and George Mat-
hews, 300 acres, North West of Staunton. Adjoining
Beverly. June 24, 1762.
Thomas Raferty, 110 acres, North side of South River of
the Shenandoah, opposite of William Patterson. Aug-
ust 18, 1762.
George Seawright, 80 acres, North River of Shenandoah.
Adjoining Josiah Cunay. December 9, 1762.
James Beard, 96 acres, North River of the Shenandoah. Ad-
joining Belshim, his own land. December 21, 1762.

## Page 20

Robert Frazer, 125 acres, South River of the Shenandoah.
Adjoining Joseph Hanna, his own land. Dec. 20, 1762.
Loftes Pullin, 55 acres, Branch of Bull Pasture, adjoining
his own land. November 11, 1762.
John Robinson, 530 acres, Buffilo Creek, a Branch of Ren-
oak (Roanoke). December 10, 1762.
John Robinson, 250 acres, Buffiol Creek, Branch of Renoak
(Roanoke). Adjoining William Graham. Mentioned
Cravans Creek. February 2, 1763.
John Robinson, 138 acres, Roanoke River. February 4, 1763
Denes Getty, 204 acres, Lees Run, a branch of Catawbu
River. December 20, 1762.

## Page 21

William Caravin, 43 acres, Roanoak River. Mentioned Carivin Creek. September 27, 1762.

James Caghey, 98 acres, Roanoke River. February 5, 1763.

Uriah Akers, 134 acres, Roanoke River. February 3, 1763.

John King, 95 acres, Middle River. May 14, 1760.

Thomas Tosh, 165 acres, Roanoke River, adjoining Malcom Campbell. February 3, 1763.

Thomas Welsh, 140 acres, Roanoke River. Mentioned Mason Creek. December 28, 1762.

James Neely, 116 acres, Campbell Creek, Branch of Roanoke. December 30, 1762.

John Neely, 25 acres, adjoining the heirs of Edward McDonald, George Robason. January 26, 1763.

## Page 22

Archebald Kyle, 120 acres, Looney Creek, Dec. 21, 1762.

James Mc Afee, 52 acres, Crigs Creek. January 28, 1763.

William Lewis, 172 acres, James River, called Back Creek. Adjoining Allen. November 3, 1762.

William Lewis, 100 acres, James River. Mentioned Allens land. November 4, 1762.

William Lewis, 200 acres, James River, November 5, 1762.

William Lewis, 110 acres, James River. November 5, 1762.

William Lewis, 148 acres, James River. November 5, 1762.

William Lewis, 187 acres, James River. November 9, 1762.

## Page 23

William Lewis, 270 acres, Head Springs of Potomack. November 10, 1762.

Thomas Lewis, 1300 acres, Jackson River. Mentioned John Miller, November 8, 1762.

Thomas Lewis, 1160 acres, Shenandoah River. Mentioned Jacob Hover, Henry Downs, Ludwrick Francisco, John Madison. April 27, 1763.

## Page 24

Agnes Cuningham, 200 acres, South Branch of Potomack. March 1761.

John Madison, 230 acres, Cub Run, adjoining Seals, Crossing the run and Waggon Road, Robert Elliot, Wood. April 12, 1763.

James Trimble, 95 acres, James River. Mentioned Camp

Mountain. February 8, 1763.

Robert Campbell, 50 acres, Halfway Creek, Jan. 2, 1763.

Malcom Allen, 48 acres, on line of his own land. February 8, 1763.

John Low, 43 acres, in forks of the James River. Adjoining James Thompson. March 10, 1763.

George Taylor, 65 acres, Irish Creek, Branch of James River. March 14, 1763.

William Lapsley, 95 acres, Forks of the James River. Adjoining Hugh Lusk. Mentioned Buffilo Creek. November 12, 1762.

### Page 25

Neil Webster, 300 acres, North Branch of James River. Adjoining John Dealiss. January 7, 1763.

George Smith, 200 acres, North Branch of James River. Adjoining George Saling. August 10, 1762.

David Timble, 140 acres, Corner to his former survey. August 13, 1762.

Robert Miller, 200 acres, James River. 1762.

George Lucas, 70 acres, Beginning corner John Dayley land. January 8, 1763.

Martin Kyser, 65 acres, James River, February 5, 1763.

John McClure, 50 acres, James River. February 5, 1763.

### Page 26

Samuel McClure, 70 acres, Fork of James River. February 10, 1763.

Malcom Allen, 70 acres, Joining his old survey. Feb. 7, 1763.

David Williams, 48 acres, beginning at a corner of his own land. Mentioned Robert Campbell. January 22, 1763.

James Logan, 48 acres, Colleirs Creek, Branch of Buffilo Creek. March 9, 1763.

Alexander McCorcle, 80 acres, Fork of James River. December 7, 1762.

Samuel Lindsey, 75 acres, James River. February 7, 1763.

Thomas Bullet, 300 acres, Jackson River. Mentioned John Robinson, Hardin, Captain Bullit. June 29, 1763.

### Page 27

John Seawright, 98 acres, Naked Creek. February 22, 1763.

Ephrain Love, 153 acres, North Fork of Joes Creek. Adjoining Daniel Harrison. January 11, 1763.

Christopher Wagoner, 150 acres, Branch of Linvils Creek. February 3, 1763.

Thomas Loocher, 141 acres, Smith Creek. Adjoining Jacob Woodley, Alexander Buchanan. Mentioned Great Road. February 3, 1763.

Thomas Loocher, 68 acres, Long Meadow Branch of North River of the Shenandoah. Adjoining Valentine Sevears, Jacob Woodly. February 3, 1763.

Francis Monsey, 145 acres, Branch of Linvils Creek. Called McCays Draft below Christopher Waggoners. Adjoining Ge. . . . Spears. February 11, 1763.

James Merrow, 154 acres, Branch of Smiths Creek, between Carrelsland and the Peaked Mountain. Feb. 3, 1763.

John Hopkins, 23 acres, Head Branch of Muddy Creek. January 11, 1763.

Jacob Rambo, 16 acres, Branch of Smiths Creek. Adjoining Philips, and his own land.

## Page 28

Archibald Hopkins, 310 acres, both sides Muddy Creek. January 10, 1763.

Robert William, 240 acres, Cub Run. Adjoining George Carpenter, William English. January 31, 1763.

Thomas More, 200 acres, Smiths Creek. Adjoining Davison, Phillips, Rambo. February 4, 1763.

Solomon Turpine, 192 acres, Dry fork of Smiths Creek. Adjoining Daniel Smith, Jeremiah Harrison. January 31, 1763.

William Shaw, 190 acres, Branch of Linvils Creek. Adjoining Christopher Wagoner. February 10, 1763.

John Phillips, 164 acres, Between Smiths Creek and Peaked Mountain. February 7, 1763.

Andrew Bird, 150 acres, Smith Creek. February 7, 1763.

Mathias Leeher, 147 acres, Linvils Creek. Adjoining Miller, his own land. February 8, 1763.

## Page 29

Daniel Smith, 75 acres, Smiths Creek. January 27, 1763.

James Bruster, 71 acres, between his line and John Stephenson. January 28, 1763.

David Robinson, 55 acres, North River of the Shenandoah. February 9, 1763.

John Haneson, 18 acres, Small Branch of Smiths Creek.

February 1, 1763.

John Gratton, 135 acres, North River of the Shenandoah. Adjoining John Hairs. Mentions and shows on plat when Pennsylvania Road crosses North River (this road leading from Indian trail at Gilberts to the Mossey Creek Country).. January 8, 1763.

Thomas Bullit, 28 acres, Jackson River. June 30, 1763.

Thomas Bullit, Andrew Lewis, and Thomas Lewis, 300 acres, Jacksons River. June 29, 1763.

### Page 30

Robert Scot, 70 acres, Stony Lick Run. Adjoining Mathew Thompson, John Davis. May 3, 1763.

John Davis, 33 acres, Collins Branch. Adjoining his own land. May 3, 1763.

John Craig, 300 acres, Cub Run. May 4, 1763.

Jacob Miller, 130 acres, Stony Run, between Shenandoah River and Peaked Mountain. May, 1763.

Frederick Stoneburg, 70 acres, branch of Stony Run. Mentioned Kertleys Survey. May 10, 1763.

Thomas Bush, 47 acres, Between Peaked Mountain and Shenandoah River. Adjoining Daniel Price. May 11, 1763.

Oldrick Herseman, 27 acres, Shenandoah River. Adjoining Lung (Long). May 12, 1763.

William Waterson, 200 acres, Naked Creek. Adjoining John King. Mentioned Kings Mill pond. November 8, 1763.

John Poage, 80 acres, Forks of James River. Adjoining his own land. March 12, 1764.

### Page 31

James Simpson and William McMunay, 160 acres, South Mountain. October 6, 1763.

James Tilford, 98 acres, South Mountain. Oct. 6, 1763.

John Adams, 94 acres, South Mountain. October 6, 1763.

William Mc . . . . . ., 33 acres, South Mountain. Oct. 6, 1763.

Mathew Mullin, 140 acres, Forks James River. Adjoining John Maxwell. October 13, 1763.

Robert Armstrong, 80 acres, Fork of James River. Adjoining his former survey on Broad Creek. Nov. 28, 1763.

James Trimble, 85 acres, South Branch Potomack, called the Crab Apple Fork. March 16, 1763.

William Hall, 45 acres, James River. Adjoining his former survey. March 2, 1764.

Thomas Paxton, 30 acres, North Branch of James River. Adjoining his own land. May 18, 1763.

## Page 32

Mathew Thompson, 65 acres, Branch Stony Lick Run. Adjoining Patrick Frazures, his own land, Hook. December 1, 1763.

Robert Hook Jr., 170 acres, head of Stony Lick Run. Adjoining Robert Hook, Mathew Thompson. December 2, 1763.

Robert Shanklin, 130 acres, Stony Lick Run. Adjoining Hooks, Mathew Thomson, land he lives on. Dec. 3, 1763.

Robert Shanklin, 235 acres, Mill Creek. Adjoining John Madison. December 3, 1763.

Mathew Thomson, 70 acres, Stony Lick Run. Adjoining his own land. December 1, 1763.

Robert Scot, 83 acres, Collins Branch. Mentioned John Davis. December 2, 1763.

Partick Barrat, 150 acres, between Shenandoah River and Peaked Mountain. Adjoining Byers. September 1, 1764.

## Page 33

James Neely, 400 acres, Roanoke River. Adjoining Greffins, Evins. February 14, 1764.

Thomas Barns, 350 acres, Buffilo Creek, Branch of Roanoke. Adjoining Malcom Campbell. February 19, 1764.

William Whiteside, 150 acres, Ronoke River. Feb. 18, 1764.

William Carleton, 90 acres, Ronoke River, Branch of Measons Creek. February 15, 1764.

William Carleton, 137 acres, Roanoke River Lick Run. Adjoining John Bryan, Samuel Brown, and his own land. February 14, 1764.

John Eager, 75 acres, Roanoke River. February 17, 1764.

Henry Forguson, 130 acres, Waters of the Roanoke. December 19, 1763.

## Page 34

William Bierd, 270 acres, Branch Roanoke River, called Creelys Branch. March 6, 1764.

James Brian, 480 acres, Waters of the Roanoke River. Adjoining Griffens. February 15, 1764.

Thomas Tosh, 254 acres, Waters of the Roanoke. Adjoining

Maleam Campbel, Uriah Akers, David Bryan, February 17, 1764.

Isreal Christian, 400 acres, Roanoke River, Buffilo Creek. Adjoining his own land. February 23, 1764.

James Robertson, 113 acres, Roanoke River. Adjoining Isaac Taylor, his own land. January 25, 1764.

William Preston, 150 acres, Buffilo Creek, Branch of the James River. Adjoining John Armstrong. January 21, 1764.

Mathias Youkam, 20 acres, Roanoke River. Feb. 11, 1764.

### Page 35

John Burress, 160 acres, Small Branch of Roanoke. Adjoining Bealy. January 26, 1764.

Hugh Mills, 129 acres, Welchman Run Branch of Roanoke. December 19, 1763.

John Smith, 98 acres, Small Branch of the James River. June 4, 1763.

William Robinson, 81 acres, Roanoke River. Adjoining John Madison, his own land. January 24, 1764.

Phillip Watkins, 26 acres, Catawba Creek, Branch of the James River. Adjoining William Richees. March 2, 1764.

Alexander Boyd, 24 acres, Roanoke River. Adjoining Joseph Loor, his own land. February 15, 1764.

Robert Young, 137 acres, Falling Spring Waters a branch of the Middle River. Adjoining Robert King. May 14, 1760.

### Page 36

James Tremble, 230 acres, Fork of James River. Adjoining Samuel McClure, Samuel Moore. May 9, 1765.

Samuel Walker, 85 acres, Forks James River. March 2, 1764.

Patrick Denney 65 acres, Fork James River. Adjoining John Hannah, Samuel Davis. September 22, 1764.

Peter Angley, 25 acres, Head Branches of Mary Creek in the South Mountain. October 24, 1764.

Michael Dockerty, 98 acres, Forks of James River. Adjoining his own land. February 18, 1759.

Robert McClenahan, 375 acres. Adjoining James McClung, Robert Campbel. Mentioned Benjamin Borden. May 29, 1765.

Arthur McClure, 35 acres, Fork of James River. Adjoining Michael Docherleis. January 29, 1761.

## Page 37

Andrew McCom, 460 acres. November 25, 1763.

John Dickinson, 217 acres, Branch of Jacksons River. June 29, 1763.

Joseph Moze, 147 acres, Branch of Cow Pasture River. June 24, 1763.

William McNiell, 159 acres, West Branch of Cooks Creek. Adjoining Craven, Hemphil. March 16, 1764.

Thomas Greeg, 140 acres, Dry Branch of Linville Creek. Adjoining Samples, Herrons, Adams, Harrison. February 16, 1764.

Edaniah Verden, 134 acres, Irish Sink Draft. Adjoining Cain Chippin, Hanison. February 16, 1764.

Henry Panninger, 131 acres, South Branch Potomack. May 29, 1765.

James Patterson, 95 acres, Middle River of the Shenandoah. Adjoining his own land and James Gambles. January 13, 1764.

## Page 38

Hugh Ross, 118 acres, Middle River of the Shenandoah. Between his own land and John Campbles. April 3, 1764.

John King, 300 acres, Naked Creek. Adjoining his own land. November 24, 1763.

William Man, 49 acres, Jackson River. March 3, 1763.

David Glen, 50 acres, North Side of the South Mountain at Rockfish Gap on a Branch of the South River. May 23, 1764.

Richard Moris, 93 acres, Jackson River. Mentioned Armsrong land. March 4, 1763.

John Harrison, 90 acres, Branch of Linvils Creek. Adjoining Ewins and his own land. February 16, 1764.

Daniel Love, 53 acres, East Fork of Cooks Creek. Between Cravens and his own land. February 15, 1764.

Michael Hogshead, 40 acres, Head of Moffets Branch, a Branch of Middle River of Shenandoah. Adjoining David Hogshead, Gilkeson, Montgomeries Corner. April 12, 1764.

Samuel Hemphills, 43 acres, East Branch Cooks Creek. Between his own and Thomas Harrison land. February 15, 1764.

## Page 39

John Blair, 19 acres, Long Glad.e Adjoining his own land,. John Andersons, James Blair. November 25, 1763.

John Riley, 37 acres, Jackson River. Adjoining Mouse land. March 5, 1763.

Samuel Henderson, 160 acres Dry River. Adjoining Hill. May 16, 1765.

John Dickson, 32 acres, Middle River. Adjoining Moffits,. Archers, and Carson. August 5, 1764.

John Cockran, 400 acres, Middle River. Adjoining his own and Burnside land. July 29, 1764.

Andrew Whitenlough, 260 acres. Place called the forest, Be-- tween Swords land and Fairfax line. Adjoining George Readers, May 6, 1765.

Rudolph Emobough, 221 acres. Place called the forest, Be- tween Swords land and Fairfax line. Adjoining George Readers, May 6, 1765.

Mathew Roads, 164 acres, place called the Forest. Adjoin- ing Henry Knaves land and above Readers. May 6, 1765.

## Page 40

Mathias Leeher, 200 acres, North fork of the Shenandoah. May 4, 1765.

Henry Knave, 118 acres, Place called the forest above Rea- ders. Adjoining Roads. May 6, 1765.

Jacob Grubb, a tract of land, North side of the Peaked Mountain on a Branch of Smiths Creek. Adjoining Harrison, Grub, his own land. May 3, 1765.

Jeremiah Harrison, 176 acres, Joining his otheer land on Smith Creek. Adjoining Turpines, Smith, Grubb. May 2, 1765.

Zebulen Harrison, a tract of land . . . . . Mentioned his father's line. May 3, 1765.

Robert McCutchen, 50 acres, Naked Creek. Adjoining Da- vid Frame, his own land. June 19, 1765.

Peter Miller, 118 acres, Between James Lards and the Peaked Mountain. States that the patent was not is- sued because of errors. March 1, 1765.

## Page 41

William Ohler (Eiler), 1900 acres, North side of Shenan- doah River, part of 3000 acres formerly surveyed to James Maxwell. August 3, 1765.

John Fulch, 420 acres, North side of the Shenandoah, part of 3000 acres formerly surveyed to James Maxwell and adjudged to William Ohler by Council. April 4, 1765.

Nicholas Huffman, 170 acres, Between the Woods Land and the Peaked Mountain. Adjoining George Huffman. April 5, 1765.

Henry Lung, 150 acres, Corner to land he lives on. April 2, 1765.

Henry Huffman, 54 acres, Beginning in a line of Dashiers land . . . . . to Fairfaxes line. February 26, 1765.

### Page 42

John Madison, 200 acres, Cooks Creek. Adjoining Joseph Cravens, his own land. April 22, 1765.

Gabriel Jones, Felix Seymore, John McCulough, Henry Heath, Luke Collins, Thomas Lewis, 1700 acres, on the mountain Between the South Fork and South Branch of the Potomack. February 22, 1765.

### Page 43

James Boggs, 235 acres, Jackson River. Adjoining Jackson and William Hamilton, and his own land. October 20, 1765.

Andrew Lewis, 280 acres, Valley of the Warm Spring Valley. June 21, 1763.

Henry Miller, 70 acres, Dry Run, near foot of the Mountain. December 30, 1765.

Henry Miller, 260 acres, between Dry Run and Naked Creek. December 30, 1765.

Jacob Bear, 550 acres, Dry Run. December 30, 1765.

William Monger, 220 acres, Naked Creek. Adjoining Evert. February 4, 1766.

George Mann, 95 acres, Stony Run. Adjoining Jacob Mann, Barnett Mann and his own land. Dec. 23, 1765.

### Page 44

Francis Kerkley, 180 acres, Naked Creek, February 5, 1766.

George Carpenter, 125 acres, East Branch of Naked Creek. February 6, 1766.

Nicholas Null, 100 acres, South Branch of Naked Creek. Adjoining Carpenter. February 6, 1766.

Martin Shoemaker, 150 acres, North Side of his own land. Adjoining Circles. May 8, 1766.

Adam Rider, 120 acres, Timber Ridge. Adjoining Mathias Roads, Circles. May 8, 1766.

James Craig, 250 acres, South River of the Shenandoah. Adjoining George Trout, Patterson. Sept. 17, 1766.

John Crum, 130 acres, West Branch of Dry River in the Mountain. Adjoining Carpenter. Feb. 6, 1766.

Page 45

John Montgomery, 30 acres, Bull Pasture River. Adjoining William Black. June 18, 1765.

James Dick, 32 acres, North Mountain. June 18, 1766.

Patrick Reiley, 45 acres, North Mountain, on the head Branches of Teases Creek. December 11, 1765.

John Jewee, 145 acres, joining Bordens. Adjoining Joseph Alexander, Samuel Paxton. April 16, 1765.

Mathew Robertson, 46 acres, joining Bordens, April 19, 1765.

Alexander Bregg, 150 acres, Forks of James River. Adjoining John Mathews, his own land, October 3, 1765.

William Naper, 40 acres, House Mountain in the Fork of James River. December 11, 1764.

William Poage, 35 acres, James River. Adjoining John Boyers, September 10, 1765.

John Sloan, 150 acres. Adjoining James Riches, William Kenney. January 20, 1765.

Page 46

William Kenney, 95 acres, Mary Creek, Branch of James River. Adjoining James Riches, John Slone. February 20, 1765.

Audley Paul, 48 acres, Adjoining his former survey. September 11, 1765.

Andrew Smithers, 75 acres, James River. Adjoining James Beats, Robert Young. September 6, 1765.

Joseph Alexander, 33 acres, joining his own land. Adjoining Bordens. February 21, 1765.

Solomon Whilby, 35 acres, James River. Sept. 5, 1765.

James Logan, 50 acres, James River. September 6, 1765.

Samuel Walker, 96 acres, James River. October 2, 1765.

Samuel Walker, 65 acres, James River. Adjoining John Buchanan. September 10, 1765.

Page 47

John Jones, 75 acres, James River. Adjoining John Buck-

hanon. September 10, 1765.
James Welsh, 50 acres, Fork of the James River. Adjoining his former survey. May 21, 1765.
Joseph Beats, 50 acres, Fork of James River. Adjoining Johnathan Whelleys. September 7, 1765.
Moses Collier, 50 acres, Fork of the James River. Adjoining his former survey. March 13, 1766.
William Bowin, 60 acres, Fork of the James River. Adjoining William Preston. February 8, 1766.
Jacob Nicholas, 120 acres, James River. February 12, 1766.
James Laurence, 300 acres, James River. Feb. 10, 1766.
James McFee, 90 acres, James River. Adjoining his own land. February 10, 1766.

### Page 48

Lewis Circle, 104 acres, at a place called the Forest. May 7, 1765.
Zubrick Conrod, 6 acres, South Branch of the Potomack. April 25, 1766.
Joseph Skidmore, 19 acres, South Branch. April 28, 1766.
William McClanahan, 50 acres, Jackson River. April 19, 1766.
Charles Power, 97 acres, Richardsons Lick Run a branch of the South Branch of the Potomack. April 26, 1766.
Jacob Harper, 40 acres, South Branch of Potomack. November 21, 1765.
John Davis, 77 acres, North Fork, of the South Branch of the Potomack called Sugartee bottom. Nov. 19, 1765.
Cornelius Bogart, 53 acres, South Branch Potomack, above Lanciscus. November 10, 1765.
Michael Peterson, 81 acres, North fork of the Potomack, five miles above Lanciscus. November 19, 1765.

### Page 49

Samuel Hirons, 97 acres, Branch of John Run, a Branch of Lenvils Creek. January 27, 1760.
Bastain Houver, 67 acres, South Branch of the Potomack. November 25, 1765.
Christopher Lowe, 98 acres, Cow Pasture River. November 28, 1766.
Nicholas Simmon, 70 acres, South Fork of the Potomack. Mentioned Green and Pickles land. November 26, 1765.
Henry Lanciscus, 299 acres, North Fork of the oPtomack.

November 18, 1765.

William McClananhaan, 25 acres, Jackson River. April 19, 1766.

Henry Panenger, 75 acres, South Branch of the Potomack.

Gabriel Coil, 12 acres, South Branch of the Potomack. May 2, 1766.

### Page 50

James Watson, 25 acres, James River. February 14, 1766.

John Hermon, 30 acres, James River. February 11, 1766.

John Neely, 60 acres, House Mountain in the fork of James River. February 12, 1766.

William Laurence, 65 acres, James River, Feb. 11, 1766.

Joseph Richeson, 90 acres, James River. February 11, 1766.

Alexander Colier, 46 acres, James River. Feb. 13, 1766.

Ritchard McGee, 50 acres, fork of James River. Adjoining William White, his own land. March 12, 1766.

John Mitchel, 60 acres, Fork of the James River. Adjoining Armstrong.

John Boyd, 20 acres, joining his old survey. Thomas Boyd. May 15, 1766.

### Page 51

Samuel Steal, 150 acres, Halfway Creek Adjoining David Steal, Boyds, McClanahan, Campbell. May 15, 1766.

Patrick Brown, 200 acres, Fork of the James River. Adjoining David Cloyds, McGavicks. October 26, 1765.

Robert Campble, 200 acres. Adjoining the line of Beverley and McCorner, Thomas Boyds. May 14, 1766.

James Laurence, 98 acres, Camp Mountain Creek, below Trimbles land. February 13, 1766.

John Walker, 95 acres, at the fork of the James River. Adjoining James Moore's. October 25, 1766.

Daniel Prentece, 80 acres, Sinking Creek Branch of the James River. February 12, 1766.

### Page 52

David Wallace, 64 acres, Forks James River. March 14, 1766.

Peter Cutwright, 60 acres, south side of the James River. Mentioned James Lawrence. September 18, 1765.

Thomas Adams, 340 acres, Warms Spring Valley. Adjoining Lewis. November 1, 1766.

George Taylor, 90 acres, Small Branch of Irish Creek. Aug-

ust 2, 1766.
Archibald Armstrong, 120 acres, Jackson River. November
5, 1766.
John Dean, 50 acres, Jackson River. November 3, 1766.
William McCah, 30 acres, Jackson River. Nov. 6, 1766.

Page 53

James Montgomery, 130 acres, James River, known by the
name of the Rich Patch. June 18, 1766.
Josiah Crawford, 42 acres, Craig Creek. October 10, 1765.
Andrew Crawford, 26 acres, James River. Adjoining John
Crawford. October 1765.
John Lowery, 47 acres, North Fork of Roanoke River. Men-
tioned Enocks Creek. October 2, 1765.
William Robinson, 60 acres, Small Branch of the Roanoke
River. May 6, 1766.
Robert Gallespey, 40 acres, North side of the James River.
June 18, 1766.
Martain Keizer, 46 acres, North side of the James River.
June 27, 1766.
John McClure, 54 acres, North side James River, at a place
called Grassy Bottom. June 28, 1766.

Page 54

Andrew Lewis, 625 acres, Roanoke River. Mentioned Bane.
Adjoining James Neely, and John Bryan. Oct. 27, 1765.
Francis Smith, 170 acres, Small Branch of Catapo. April
22, 1765. N. B. This was formerly surveyed for Samuel
Thompson and for him kept back til October 22, 1766.
Thomas Bullet, 370 acres, Falling Spring Valley. December
2, 1766.
Thomas Bullet, 280 acres, Falling Spring Valley. Adjoining
John Dickinson. December 1, 1766.
Thomas Bullet, 250 acres, Warm Spring Mountain. Dec-
ember 2, 1766.
Thomas Bullet, 220 acres, Sinking Spring Valley. Decem-
ber 2, 1766.

Page 55

Thomas Bullet, 220 acres, Warm Spring Valley. November
20, 1766.
Thomas Bullet, 98 acres, Warm Spring Valley. December
3, 1766.
Gabriel Jones, 270 acres, Warm Spring Valley. December

4, 1766.

Gabriel Jones, 350 acres, Warm Spring Valley. December 4, 1766.

Gabriel Jones, 290 acres, Warm Spring Valley, December 4, 1766.

Andrew Lewis, 98 acres, Warm Spring Valley. October 29, 1766.

Andrew Lewis, 45 acres, Warm Spring Valley. November 3, 1766.

## Page 56

Thomas Nelson, George Wilson, John Madison, Seronima Ramley, Abraham Smith, John Smera, John Paoge, Adam Weese, James Huston, Jacob Weese, Sampson Mathews, Michael Thom, Daniel Smith, Anthony Cooper, Alexander McClanahan, Tobias Thom, David Scot, Henry Shepler, Robert Lowthee, John Bryan, George Bush, and Hermen Shoe, 1080 acres, South Fork Potomack River, November 15, 1765.

Andrew Bird, John Phillips, John Poage, John McAnelly, Thomas George, John Phillips Jr., and James Daubin, 1500 acres. South River, both sides of the Rockfish Gap Road. March 26, 1766.

Valentine Castle, 87 acres, Richardsons Run, a Branch of the Potomack. April 26, 1766.

## Page 57

John Finley, 238 acres, Middle River of the Shenandoah. February 7, 1766.

William and Samuel Kindhead (Kinkaid), 337 acres, Jackson River. Adjoining Dean. April 19, 1766.

Jacob Pichle, 70 acres, South Branch of the Potomack. November 25, 1765.

Adam, Jacob, and John Wees, 254 acres, South Branch of the Potomack. Adjoining Thomas Parsons, Green. November 14, 1765.

William Crawford, 120 acres, Middle River of the Shenanandoah. May 2, 1766.

William Crow, 45 acres, South Branch of the Potomack. April 25, 1766.

Isaac Kennerly, 120 acres, South River of the Shenandoah. July 9, 1766.

## Page 58

Peter Venimon, 128 acres, South Branch of the Potomack. April 26, 1766.

John Jorden, 90 acres, Between South Branch and Bull Pasture. May 10, 1766.

William Robertson, 90 acres, Middle River Branch of the Shenandoah. Adjoining Anderson's, and his own land. February 18, 1766.

Michael Wiltfeng. 111 acres, South Branch of the Potomack. April 24, 1766.

Daniel McNeare, 96 acres, Middle River of the Shenandoah. February 7, 1766.

Conrod Good, 44 acres, South Branch of the Potomack. April 24, 1766.

John Schooleraft, 53 acres, South Branch of the Potomack. December 11, 1766.

## Page 59

Mathias Schooleraft, 130 acres, South Branch of the Potomack. December 11, 1766.

William Robertson and Andrew Russel, 193 acres, on the Long Meadows. Adjoining James Andreson, his own land. November 27, 1766.

Thomas Wilmouth, 130 acres, South Branch of the Potomack. December 4, 1766.

Joseph Skidmore, 34 acres, South Branch of the Potomack. December 9, 1766.

Thomas Deverick, 34 acres, Cow Pasture River. Mentioned Estill Rodd.

Michael Oliboust, 130 acres, Crab Apple Waters. Mentioned Cunningham. December 9, 1766.

Anthony Johnston, 72 acres, Cow Pasture River. December 12, 1766.

Thomas Spencer, 98 acres, Briery Branch of North River. November 7, 1766.

## Page 60

Michael Bush, 375 acres, South Branch of the Potomack. December 10, 1766.

Adam Harper, 126 acres, Crab Apple Waters. Dec. 9, 1766.

John Gum, 72 acres, Crab Apple Waters, Dec. 9, 1766.

Barnet Lynch, 182 acres, Crab Apple Waters. Dec. 10, 1766.

Andrew Lewis, 175 acres, Jackson River. Adjoining James

Fitz. October 30, 1766.

Andrew Lewis, 96 acres, Warm Spring Mountain. October 29, 1766.

## Page 61

John Stephenson, 335 acres, Beginning at the corner of his own land and adjoining Archibald Huston's. December 12, 1766.

Charles Lewis, 30 acres, Cow Pasture River. Nov. 4, 1766.

James Bogg, 112 acres, Jackson River. Nov. 1, 1766.

Andrew Lewis, 200 acres, Jackson River. Oct. 28, 1766.

Francis Smith, 400 acres Roanoke River. Adjoining Israel Cristian, Thomas Barns, mentioned Great Road. February 21, 1767.

## Page 62

David Robison, 50 acres, House Mountain. Adjoining John Neely. February 4, 1767.

Moses Cunningham, 60 acres, Carrs Creek. Adjoining his own land, Jacob Cunningham. February 4, 1767.

Halbert McClure, 65 acres, Fork of the James River. February 5, 1767.

John Cresinburg, 70 acres, Branch of Colliers Creek. February 5, 1767.

James McCalester, 22 acres House Mountain. Feb. 8, 1767.

James Logan 38 acres, Fork of the James River. Adjoining Trimble. February 10, 1767.

James Trimble, 150 acres, Fork of the James River. Adjoining James Trimble. February 10, 1767.

Peter Kelly, 240 acres, James River. Adjoining James Barton. March 10, 1767.

Andrew Smithers, 200 acres, Forks of the James River. February 10, 1767.

James Shanks, 50 acres, Carrs Creek. Adjoining Moses Cunningham. February 4, 1766.

## Page 63

James Ward, 160 acres, Jackson River. October 30, 1766.

William Christian, 385 acres, James River. Nov. 10, 1766.

William Christian, 45 acres, James River. Nov. 10, 1766.

William Gilespy, 50 acres, James River. Nov. 8, 1766.

John Hamilton, 125 acres, Jackson River. Adjoining Jackson. October 30, 1766.

Thomas Carpender, 50 acres, South side of the James River. November 6, 1766.

David Tate, 80 acres, James River. November 7, 1766.

Thomas Kelley, 35 acres, James River. November 7, 1766.

John Dickinson, 22 acres, Cowpasture River. Nov. 26, 1766.

## Page 64

Jeremiah Seely, 200 acres, Falling Spring Valley. December 1, 1766.

James Galespy, 50 acres, Jackson River. Adjoining Robert Galespy. November 8, 1766.

Wallace Estill, 360 acres, Jackson River. December 9, 1766.

John Estill, 150 acres, Newfound Creek. Dec. 13, 1766.

Thomas Adams, 235 acres, Calfpasture River. Adjoining William Kinkade. March 25, 1767.

Thomas Adams, 190 acres, Calfpasture River. March 27, 1767.

## Page 65

James Barton, 98 acres, James River. February 11, 1767.

Malcom Allen, 65 acres, Adjoining his own land. February 15, 1767.

John Taylor, 11 acres, South side of the James River. Adjoining Malcom Allen. February 17, 1767.

Johnathan Whittey, 48 acres, James River. February, 1767

Malcom Allen, 100 acres, James River. Adjoining John Taylor. February 17, 1767.

Samuel Gibson, 46 acres, Buffilo Creek. February 18, 1767.

Robert Campbell, 46 acres, Fork of the James River. Adjoining Samuel Hunter, William Davis. Feb. 18, 1767.

James Clencey, 125 acres James River. February 18, 1767.

## Page 66

William Davis, 45 acres, Buffilo Creek. February 18, 1767.

Samuel Gibson, 50 acres, Fork of James River. February 19, 1767.

Samuel Gibson, 70 acres, North side of Short Mountain. February 19, 1767.

Joseph Long, 45 acres, joining his old survey. Feb. 20, 1767.

James Huston and James Trimble, 30 acres North Branch of the James River. March 3, 1767.

John Wallace, 150 acres, North side of the James River. March 5, 1767.

Mathew Hare, 80 acres, Fork of James River. March 7, 1767.

John Skelton, 50 acres, Fork of the James River. March 9,. 1767.

Benjamin Estill, 65 acres, on James River. March 9, 1767.

### Page 67

William Chapman, 50 acres, Fork of the James River. Adjoining Joseph Dennis. March 9, 1767.

Peter Kelley, 50 acres, Forks of the James River. March 10, 1767.

George Dockerty, 50 acres, Forks of the James River. Adjoining William Crawford. March 11, 1767.

John Low, 95 acres, Fork of the James River. March 11, 1767.

Daniel Gooding, 96 acres, James River. Adjoining Greenlee March 11, 1767. N. B. with the colledge to this place before 1769. Thomas Lewis S. A. Co.

Hugh Gillespey, 85 acres, Cowpasture River. May 29, 1767

William Ramsey, 85 acres beginning at a corner of his old survey. September 24, 1767.

William Craig, 65 acres, Coypasture River. June 2, 1767.

### Page 68

William Ray, 24 acres, Fork of the James River. Adjoining Henry Larkins. April 4, 1767.

Alexander Dunlap, 90 acres, Calfpasture River. Adjoining William Jamason. June 6, 1767.

Samuel Moore, 80 acres, James River. Adjoining his own land, James Trimble. April 6, 1767.

Patrick McColm, 98 acres, Forks of the James River. Adjoining McKorkle, his own land. April 6, 1767.

Samuel McClure, 60 acres, Forks of the James River. Adjoining his own land, William Foster, John Poage. April 9, 1767.

Jean Mouldrough, 30 acres, Forks James and Cowpasture River. Adjoining Grahams.

Andrew Hamilton, 185 acres, Calfpasture River. Adjoining John Kinkade, James Campbell, June 4, 1767.

### Page 69

James Campbell, 154 acres, Calfpasture River. Adjoining John Kinkade, Andrew Hamilton. June 4, 1767.

Sampson and George Mathews, 69 acres, Cowpasture River June 3, 1767.

Charles Lewis, 125 acres, place called the Red Hole. June 1, 1767.

Samuel McMurray, 65 acres, Cowpasture River. May 28, 1767.

James Gay, 125 acres, Dickesons Mill Draft, a Branch of the Cowpasture River. May 30, 1767.

James McDowel, 150 acres, Forks of the James River. Adjoining James Trimble, Samuel Moore, April 9, 1767.

Jean Mouldrough, 33 acres, South side of James River. May 27, 1767.

## Page 70

James Campbell, 85 acres, Calfpasture River. June 4, 1767

William Hugart, 135 acres, James River. Mentioned John Robinson. May 26, 1767.

William Thompson, 93 acres, Cowpasture River. May 27, 1767.

Alexander Croket, 97 acres, Cowpasture River. June 5, 1767.

Thomas Bullet, 100 acres, Hot Springs. Adjoining Gabriel Jones. December 3, 1767.

Andrew Lewis, 45 acres, Hot Springs. Adjoining Thomas Adams. December 3, 1767.

## Page 71

John Crawford, Sr., 136 acres, James River. July 25, 1767.

John Crawford, Jr., 40 acres, James River. July 27, 1767.

William Crawford, 44 acres, James River. July 23, 1767.

Thomas Dooly, 214 acres, Branch of the James River. February 4, 1767.

Abraham Dooly, 80 acres, Branch of the James River. February 4, 1767.

James Neely, 445 acres, Roanoke River. February 18, 1767

## Page 72

John Mills, 345 acres, Branch of the James River. Adjoining Col. P. Smith, William Borland, James Borland. February 10, 1767.

John Mills, 254 acres, Looney Creek. Adjoining John Looney. February 12, 1767.

William McMullan, 215 acres, Roanoke River. June 6, 1767

Robert Neely, 152 acres, Roanoke River. Adjoining Archibald Graham, William Christian. August 7, 1767.

John Madison, 104 acres, Roanoke River, Jan. 27, 1767.

Joseph Crab, 104 acres, Roanoke River. September 26, 1766
James Caghey, 95 acres, Roanoke River. Adjoining John
Egar, February 20, 1767.

### Page 73

Dennes Getty, 320 acres, Branch of the Catawba. September 12, 1766.
John Clark, 210 acres, Branch of the James River. February 13, 1766.
William Snodgrass, 120 acres, Branch of James River. September 13, 1767.
John Conley, 80 acres, South side of the James River. June 20, 1766.
Benjamin Paulson, 66 acres, North Fork of the Roanoke River. June 8, 1767.
Samuel Lawrance, 60 acres, Branch of the James River.
James McMillin, 46 acres, Branch of James River. June 10, 1767.
James Moore, 44 acres, Branch of Looney Creek. September 20, 1766.

### Page 74

Mathew Emocks, 395 acres, Branch of the Roanoke River. Adjoining Henry Forguson. June 6, 1767.
David Magee, 212 acres, Branch of Roanoke River. Adjoining William Magee. June 6, 1767..
Isaac Bellangee, 210 acres, Branch of Craig Creek. July 30 1767.
John McNeel, 280 acres, Roanoke River. Adjoining Peter Evenson. February 17, 1767.
John Mellon, 240 acres, Roanoke River. Adjoining Daniel Evens, Samuel Andrew, William Terry. Mentioned Great Road. May 30, 1767.
Thomas Smith, 198 acres, Roanoke River. Adjoining William Terry. September 24, 1766.
George and James Alexander, 80 acres, Roanoke River. September 25, 1766.
Jasper Farry, 165 acres, Roanoke River. Adjoining William Farry. 1766.

### Page 75

Babtist Armstrong, 304 acres, Roanoke River. May 28, 1767.
Nathaniel Evens, 185 acres, Roanoke River. Adjoining

Griffins. May 29, 1767.
James Robertson, 184 acres, Roanoke River. Jan. 28, 1767.
Richard Reed, 135 acres, Roanoke River. Adjoining John
Thompson. May 27, 1767.
Hugh Crocket, 87 acres, South Fork of the Roanoke River.
Adjoining John Madison. June 4, 1767.
Thomas Akers, 52 acres, Roanoke River. May 28, 1767.
James Roberston, 50 acres, Roanoke River. June 4, 1767.
Francis Liver, 50 acres, Catawba Creek. Adjoining James
McCown. June 20, 1767.

Page 76

Francis Smith, 285 acres, Cataba Creek. Adjoining McRo-
berts, William Moore, William Hutchison. September
18, 1766.
Peter Dyerly, 365 acres, Roanoke River. June 2, 1767.
Patrick Sharky, 15 acres, James River. July 24, 1767.
Simeon Dehart, 90 acres, Craigs Creek, Branch of the
James River. Adjoining Israel Christian, Estate Col.
Patton. July 25, 1767.
John Robinson, 83 acres, Deer Run. Branch of Roanoke
River. Adjoining Thomas Evens. June 5, 1767.
Thomas Tosh, 63 acres, North Branch of Roanoke River.
Adjoinging Elizabeth Robinson. 1767.
James Montgomery, 60 acres, Rich Patch Mountain. July
22, 1767.

Page 77

John Bradley, 110 acres, Creely Branch of Roanoke River.
Adjoinging Mathew Emock. May 26, 1767.
Andrew and William Miller, 103 acres, Catawba Creek. Ad-
joining Samuel McRobert, John Miller. Feb. 14, 1767.
Robert Brackinridge, 54 acres, South side of James River.
August 4, 1767.
Joseph McMustray, 54 acres, Craig Creek. August 1, 1767.
William Colly, 50 acres, North side of James River. July
23, 1767.
William McClellon, 30 acres, Looney Creek. Adjoining
John McClellon. September 19, 1767.
Patrick Sharky, 10 acres South side of James River. July
24, 1767.

Page 78

Robert Ritchie, 25 acres, North Fork of Roanoke River.

30 ABSTRACT OF SURVEYS

Adjoining Robert McGee, Joseph McDonald, John Heaven. November 6, 1767.

JohnPoage, 27 acres, Adjoining Robert Stepsenson. Mentioned the Stone Meeting house. May 13, 1760.

James Robertson, 135 acres, South Fork of Roanoke. November 8, 1767.

John Robinson, 64 acres, North Fork of Roanoke River. November 7, 1767.

John Robinson, 175 acres, Buffilo Branch of Roanoke River Adjoining Francis Graham, Robert Branchinridge. September 11, 1767.

John Robinson, 110 acres, Roanoke. Adjoining Ingles. June 6, 1767.

John Robinson, 135 acres, Roanoke. Adjoining William Handley. Mentioned Ingles Mill Creek.. Nov. 9, 1767.

Page 79

John Robinson, 69 acres, Fork of Roanoke River. Adjoining William Inglish, Ingle. November 7, 1767.

William Yully, 93 acres, Potts Creek. Branch of James October 5, 1767.

William Yully, 139 acres, Both sides James River. October 15, 1767.

Robert Brackinridge, 1108 acres, Roanoke River. Adjoining Peter Evens, John Robinson, William Garvin, Carvin, Neal McNeel. September 10, 1767.

Edward McMullin, 56 acres, Dunlaps. Branch of James River. Adjoining Col. Lewis. October 13, 1767.

Page 80

Edward McMullen, 251 acres, Dunlaps Creek. Branch of James River. October 12, 1767.

Francis Smith, 360 acres, Roanoke. Adjoining Peter Dyerly and Isaac Taylor. June 4, 1767.

Francis Smith, 150 acres, Dills Creek, Branch of Roanoke River. Adjoining Joseph Crab. February 18, 1767.

Lopher Carpenter, 50 acres, James River. October 16, 1767

Joseph Carpenter, Sr., 115 acres, Potts Creek, Branch of James River. October 6, 1767.

Solomon Carpenter, 50 acres, Potts Creek. Branch of the James River. October 16, 1767.

Page 81

Andrew Lewis, 325 acres, Dunlaps Creek. October 13, 1767

Andrew Lewis, 525 acres, Dunlaps Creek. Mentioned Indian Road. October 13, 1767.

William Lewis, 524 acres, Dunlaps Creek. Adjoining William Hugart. October 10, 1767.

William Preston, 96 acres, Craigs Creek, Branch of James River. Adjoining Hartsough, John Potts. July 30, 1767

### Page 82

William Preston, 1430 acres, Potts Creek, Branch of the James River. Mentioned a Beaver dam, Hurricanes Land. October 6, 1767.

### Page 83

William Preston, 350 acres, Potts Creek, Branch of the James River. October 3, 1767.

Solomon Carpenter, 43 acres, Potts Creek, Branch of James River. October 7, 1767.

Samuel Crockett, 57 acres, Roanoke River. Adjoining William Robinson, Samuel Robinson. November 13, 1767.

Daniel Allen, 54 acres, North Branch of Roanoke River. Adjoining Wellson. June 6, 1767.

Joseph Colvin, 70 acres, Roanoke River. December 9, 1767.

Samuel Crokett, 40 acres, South Fork of Roanoke River. November 11, 1767.

### Page 84

Israel Christian, 447 acres, Roanoke River. Adjoining William Cowan, Patterson, William Grohonis, Rosanna Christian, Hugh Mills. August 7, 1767.

Benjamin Paulson, 135 acres, North Fork of Roanoke River. June 7, 1767.

James McMillin, 135 acres, Catawba Creek. Adjoining John Donalley. June 9, 1767.

James Neely, 200 acres, Roanoke. Mentioned Huffs Path December 10, 1767.

### Page 85

Jacob Brown, 50 acres, North Fork of Roanoke River. Adjoining Thomas Tosh. June 5, 1767.

Patrick Buchanan, 54 acres, Dunlaps Creek. Branch of the James River. Adjoining Thomas Man. October 13, 1767

Andrew Wood, 185 acres, North Fork of Roanoke River. November 5, 1767.

James Barnett, 54 acres, Roanoke. December 8, 1767.

John McNeil, 355 acres, Roanoke. Adjoining Evans, Barnes. December 14, 1767.

Moses Mellecan, 70 acres, Roanoke. December 12, 1767.

James Caghey, 77 acres, Roanoke. Adjoining Moses Mell-
ecans. December 12, 1767.

## Page 86

John Seawright, 188 acres, Naked Creek, Adjoining, Hugh
Campbell. 1767.

James Hogshead, 89 acres, Moffets Branch. Adjoining Thomas Bradshaw. February 27, 1767.

Paul Custard, 171 acres, Brocks Gap. Adjoining John Miller. February 12, 1767.

Uriah Humble, 134 acres, Brocks Gap. Adjoining Martin
Humble. February 12, 1767.

Thomas Bradshaw, 25 acres Moffets Branch. Adjoining Alexander Gardner. April 15, 1767.

Peter Runimes, 126 acres, North side of the Shenandoah
River. May 29, 1767.

Henry Null, 150 acres, South side of Naked Creek. Branch
of the Shenandoah River. May 28, 1767.

Conrod Peter Fesh, 86 acres, North side of the Shenandoah
River. May 29, 1767.

Jacob Runkle, 57 acres, North side of the Shenandoah River. Adjoining Burks. May 30, 1767.

## Page 87

William Reash, 68 acres, Calfpasture River. June 2, 1767.

Samuel McFeters, 39 acres, Mossey Creek, April 23, 1767.

Daniel Price, 85 acres, North side of the Shenandoah River. Adjoining Judy Burk. May 29, 1767.

Jarred Ewin, 51 acres, Briery Branch. Adjoining John Mc-
Vea. April 22, 1767.

Mathew Frame, 56 acres, North side of Dry River. April
23, 1767.

John McVea, 113 acres, Between Beaver Creek and Briery
Branch. Adjoining Henry Black. April 22, 1767.

William Johnston, 230 acres, Middle River, Adjoining
Campbell, Athen Connely. April 20, 1767.

Reuben Harrison, 48 acres, Branch of Smith Creek. April
15, 1767.

Robert Campbell, 55 acres, Middle River. Adjoining William Johnston, Cohnan. April 17, 1767.

John Nicholas, 44 acres, North side of Moffets Branch. April 15, 1767.

### Page 88

Evon Thomas, 97 acres, Linvil Creek. Adjoining James Green. February 19, 1767.

James Thomas, 122 acres, Ceder Run. Adjoining Samuel Nicholas, John Beailie. February 18, 1767.

John Phips, 83 acres, Brocks Creek. Adjoining Kennely, Corner, Haverstick. February 17, 1767.

John Jackson, 215 Ceder Run, Branch of the Shenandoah River below John Thomases land. Adjoining Shoemaker. February 17, 1767.

John Badee, 58 acres, Ceder Run. Adjoining John Nicholos Haverstick, February 18, 1767.

Martin Humble, 89 acres, both sides of the River, Brocks Gap. February 12, 1767.

Samuel Corner, 114 acres, North side of Brocks Creek. February 14, 1767.

Robert Carr, 178 acres, Draft of Linvil's creek. Adjoining Riddle. February 18, 1767.

Samuel Nicholas, 69 acres, South Branch of Brocks Creek. February 17, 1767.

### Page 89

Alexander Walker, 413 acres, Lying on Little Run. Adjoining McClenahan, Reaburn, Conley, April 4, 1765.

Henry Cresswell, 135 acres, Middle River of the Shenandoah. Adjoining John Elliot, Crawford. Jan. 28, 1767.

John Grattan, 540 acres, North River of the Shenandoah between Hugh Campbell and John Hairs. Adjoining James Trotters. September 1, 1767.

John Dickison, 18 acres, Cowpasture River. 1767.

George Lewis, 10 acres, Middle River of the Shenandoah. September 22, 1767.

### Page 90

John Davison, 225 acres, Dry River. Adjoining Abraham Smith, Stephenson. November 6, 1767.

John Hinds, 330 acres. Muddy Creek and Dry River. Mentioned Janes Anderson, William McMullen. September 3. 1767.

Andrew Johnston and Michael Aberman, 148 acres, Seneca Creek, Branch of North Branch of South Branch of the Potomack. October 29, 1767.

Andrew Johnston and Jacob Aberman, 152 acres, South Branch of the Potomack adjoining Mallow. October 23, 1767.

Page 91

Andrew Johnston, 960 acres, between Mole Hill and Muddy Creek. Adjoining Hinton, and his own land. April 18, 1768.

Jacob Aberman, Jr., 71 acres, North of South Branch of the Potomack adjoining Leonard Simmons, John Aberman. October 30, 1767.

William Aberman, 26 acres, South Branch of the Potomack. October 3, 1767.

John Warmley, 384 acres, Mole Hill Draft, a Branch of of Cooks Creek, Adjoining Daniel Harrison. December 2, 1767.

Page 92

Samuel Wilson, 167 acres, straight Fork of the Potomack. February 19, 1768.

Samuel Wilson, 63 acres, Bull Pasture. February 16, 1768.

Samuel Wilson 97 acres, Fork of Jackson River. February 20, 1768.

Samuel Wilson, 66 acres, Fork of Bull Pasture River. February 16, 1768.

Samuel Wilson, 62 acres, Fork of the Potomack and Crab River. February 19, 1768.

William Shannon, 77 acres, North River of Shenandoah. February 26, 1768.

William Shannon, 94 acres, head Branches of Cooks Creek, Between William Ewins and John Herdman. February 26, 1768.

Page 93

Adam Stepsenson, 284 acres, Mossey Creek adjoining Samuel Feature, Sample, Col. Stephenson. Feb. 27, 1768.

John Poage, 284 acres South Branch of the Potomack, adjoiinng Shelton. November 6, 1767.

John Leaburn, 329 acres, Middle River of the Shenandoah adjoining Andrew Ralston, Rankins. Jan. 28, 1768.

Robert Gragg, 513 acres. Mentioned William Humphery, William Wilson. February 25, 1768.

Page 94

James Marshall, 187 acres, Brocks Gap. Adjoining Miller,

Richard Ticktum. February 11, 1767.
William Gragg, 71 acres, Hunters Gully. a Branch of Cooks
Creek. Adjoining Patrick Quins, Johnston. Dec 4, 1767
David Bill, 250 acres, Bull Pasture River. Adjoining Bot-
kins, Charles Hays Roots. February 15, 1768.
Henry Reaburn, 293 acres, betwixt Jennings and Moffets
Branches. Adjoining William Custal, Michael Hogs-
head. 1768.
John Beard, 25 acres, Jennings Branch.

## Page 95

William Magee, 167 acres, North Fork of Roanoke. Ad-
joining David Magee. June 8, 1767.
James Bates, 200 acres, Roanoke. December 7, 1768.
Robert Eliot, 170 acres, South Fork of Roanoke. December
9, 1767.
Robert Eliot, 87 acres, South Fork of Roanoke. November
12, 1767.
Jeremiah Seeley, 75 acres, Dunlaps Creek Branch of the
James River. October 13, 1767.
Moses Millican, 54 acres, Roanoke. December 12, 1767.

## Page 96

Peter Wright, 60 acres, both sides of the James River. Oct-
ober 8, 1767.
Dursy Packett, 195 acres, Cataba Creek, adjoining Mullens
June 9, 1767.
Thomas Rogers, 225 acres, Looney Creek. Adjoining James
Moore, William McClellon. August 29, 1767.
James Bryans, 190 acres, Roanoke. Adjoining William
Bryan. December 7, 1767.
Francis Graham, 140 acres, Roanoke. Adjoining John Rob-
inson. August 7, 1767.
Joseph McMurbry, 27 acres, Craigs Creek, Branch of the
James River. Adjoining Robert Williams. July 31, 1767

## Page 97

John Thomson, 190 acres, Roanoke. Adjoining William
Thomson. May 27, 1767.
John Willis, 50 acres, Cataba Creek. Adjoining David Mit-
chell, James Alisons, James Snodgrass. Sept. 15, 1767
Gilbert Marshall, 160 acres, Roanoke. December 10, 1767.
Jacob Passinger, 115 acres, Indian Draft of the James

River. October 15, 1767.

Andrew Boyd, 94 acres, Roanoke River. Adjoining Samuel Brown. September 7, 1767.

William Ingles, 53 acres. North Fork Roanoke. Adjoining Thomas Ingles. November 7, 1767.

## Page 98

John Humphreys, 130 acres, Potts Creek. Branch of the James River. October 6, 1767.

Thomas Evans, 54 acres, South Fork Roanoke. November 12, 1767.

Amos Evins, 143 acres, Douth Fork Roanoke. Nov. 12, 1767

James Wilson, 26 acres, Willsons Creek, Branch of the James River. July 23, 1767.

James Wilson, 110 acres, Potts Creek, Branch of the James River. October 7, 1767.

## Page 99

Benjamin Esstill, 344 acres, North side of James River. October 25, 1767.

John Eager, 98 acres, Branch of Roanoke River. Adjoiinng James Cogheys. February 25, 1767.

Thomas Rowland, 270 acres, Spreading Spring Draft, Branch of the James River. February 26, 1768.

James Laughlin, 136 acres, Branch of Roanoke River, Ad- ·joining Thomas Price. February 13, 1768.

John Laughlin, 54 acres, Branch of Roanoke River. Ad- joining Thomas Price. February 13, 1768.

James Caghey, 140 acres, Branch of Roanoke River, Ad- joining William Cox.

William Tany, 150 acres, Branch of Roanoke River. Febru- ary 1, 1768.

Drusy Pickett, 24 acres, Craig Creek. March 18, 1768.

## Page 100

John Buckhanan, 330 acres, North side of the James River Mentioned Cherry Tree Botton, crossed Purgatory Creek, March 2, 1768.

Robert Poage, 44 acres, Branch of Roanoke River. Febru- ary 2, 1768.

John Boreland, 400 acres, Branch of Roanoke River. Feb- ruary 17, 1768.

Thomas Mann, 117 acres, Dunlaps Creek. October 12, 1767.

John Moor, 135 acres, Branch of the James River. February 25, 1768.

Reece Bowin, 67 acres, branch of the Roanoke River. Mentioned Great Road. February 17, 1768.

John Marton, 70 acres, Branch of Roanoke River. December 9, 1767.

Page 101

Thomas Price, 87 acres, Roanoke River. February 13, 1768

Andrew Lewis, 570 acres, Roanoke River. Mentioned Henry Brown, and Thomas Walker. January 29, 1767.

John Henderson, 100 acres, Calfpasture River. Adjoining Samuel Henderson, William Smith, McCutchins. February 3, 1768.

John Binson, 159 acres, Head drafts of East Branch of Cooks Creek. Adjoining Rutherfords survey. May 5, 1768.

Joseph Rutherford, 165 acres, East Branch of Cooks Creek May 5, 1768.

Joseph Rutherford, 193 acres, North side of Eliots Run, a Branc hof Cubb Run. Mentioned Eliots land. May 5, 1768.

Page 102

Frederick Stull, 193 acres, Stulls Run Branch of South River. Mentioned Patterson. May 3, 1768.

Jacob Lingle, 154 acres, May 10, 1768.

Daniel Smith, 15 acres, Adjoining Rutherford and his own land. May 5, 1768.

John Deniston, 125 acres, Mill Creek. Adjoining Shanklins. Mentioned Scotts Run and North River. Nov. 6, 1767.

Mathew Harrison, 1150 acres, North River of the Shenandoah. Mentioned Woods land, Hughes land, Seahorns land in Fairfaxes Boundary line. December 2, 1768.

John Binson, 220 acrers, North River of the Shenandoah. Mentioned Fairfax Boundry line, Woods land. December 1, 1768.

Page 103

Moses Ofreal, 560 acres, Middle River of the Shenandoah. Mentioned Beverly Manor, Walter Trimble, William Bell, Robert Wallace. November 25, 1767.

William Gwynn, 320 acres, Bullpasture River. Adjoining Barnabe Mathew. February 23, 1768.

Benjamin Kinley, 354 acres, Anthonys Springs Branch of

Linvils Creek, Adjoining Jessie Harrison, John Gordon. November 23, 1768.

William Jordan, 90 acres, Cowpasture River. November 8, 1768.

### Page 104

John Hannah, 98 acres, Fork James River. Nov. 7, 1767.

John Hannah, 120 acres, Buffilo Creek in Fork of James River. Adjoining Janes Young. November 6, 1767.

George Dockery, 70 acres, Fork of James River. October 23, 1767.

Michael Dockerty, 75 acres, Fork of the James. Adjoining Benjamin Watson. October 22, 1767.

Robert Barnett, 26 acres, Jackson River. Adjoining William Grins. December 3, 1767.

Robert Rush, 20 acres, January 6, 1767.

John Rush, 87 acres. Adjoining Robert Campbell. Mentioned Beverleys patent line. January 7, 1768.

William Grins, 38 acres, Jackson River. December 4, 1767.

### Page 105

Hugh Miller, 220 acres, Bullpasture River. Dec. 10, 1767.

Robert Campbell, 150 acres, September 29, 1767.

Solomon Whitley, 110 acres, Fork James River. November 4, 1767.

Samuel Walker, 185 acres, Fork of the James River. October 22, 1767.

William McCutchion, 150 acres, January 8, 1768.

David Frame, 210 acres, Jackson River adjoining William Warwick, December 9, 1767.

John Miller, 90 acres, Branch of Bullpasture River. December 12, 1767.

Robert Young, 130 acres, Fork of the James River, Adjoining John Hannah, Edward Pharis, James Brat. February 7, 1767.

### Page 106

Isabella Robinson, 280 acres, Forks of the James River. Adjoining William Crawford, Greenlee. October 28, 1767

James Michel, 370 acres, North side of North Mountain. Adjoining Bell. January 4, 1767.

Benjamin Kimsey, 94 acres, Walkers Creek. Adjoining Borden, James Buchanan, John Buchanan. Jan. 6, 1767

James Mitchel, 95 acres, Walkers Creek. Adjoining John

Brill, John Bush, January 5, 1767.
Benjamin Kimsey, 150 acres, North Mountain. Adjoining
James Mitchel. January 6, 1767.
Thomas Wilson, 170 acres. Adjoining Moore, Moses Collins
November 6, 1767.

Page 107

William Myas, 180 acres, Jackson River. Dec. 9, 1767.
David Frame, 98 acres, James River. December 9, 1767.
Daniel Goodwin, 170 acres, Possum Creek in the South
Mountain. October 27, 1767.
John Summres, 85 acres, Fork of the James River. November 4, 1767.
James Miller, 75 acres, Bullpasture River. Dec. 12, 1767.
Nathaniel Evans, 75 acres, Fork of the James River. Adjoining Mathews, John Heckman. December 29, 1767.
John McKinzey, 90 acres, Fork of the James River. Adjoining Hutton.. October 29, 1767.
George Campbell, 96 acres, Elk Creek. Branch of the James
River. October 28, 1767.
Henry Lachens, 50 acres, North Branch of the James River. Adjoining George Salling. December 29, 1767.
John Greenlee, 40 acres, James River. Oct. 28, 1767.

Page 108

Christian Godfrey Milleron, 60 acres, North Branch of the
James River. Adjoining James McClung, Widow Berryford. October 30, 1767.
James Simpson, 70 acres. Adjoining John Noble, William
McBride. December 28, 1767.
James Burnside, 75 acres, Bullpasture River. Adjoining
William Martens. December 12, 1767.
David Lytle, 38 acres, Fork of the James River. Adjoining
David White, Christian Godfrey, Milleron, Edmond
Crump. October 30, 1767.
James Allison, 50 acres, Fork of the James River. Adjoining James Trimble. February 22, 1768.
Alexander Gilespy, 96 acres, Jackson River. Dec. 1, 1767.
Dawson Wade, 24 acres, Bullpasture River. Dec. 11, 1767.
Stephen Arnold, 350 acres, South side of the James River.
Adjoining John Hall. May 4, 1768.

Page 109

Stephen Arnold, 190 acres, Elk Creek Branch of the James

River. October 23, 1767.

Benjamin Kimsey, 130 acres, Martins Draft. Adjoining John Rusk. January 5, 1768.

Benjamin Kimsey, 50 acres, Fork of the James River. April 15, 1768.

John Rusk, 310 acres, Calfpasture River. Adjoining John Rusk Senior, Archibald Armstrong. April 5, 1768.

William Porter, 72 acres, Forks of the James River. April 15, 1768.

## Page 110

Samuel Lawrence, 50 acres, James River. Adjoining George Givens. April 23, 1768.

Archibald Raigh, 98 acres, North Mountain. Adjoining Bordens patent. April 6, 1768.

Nathaniel Evans, 30 acres, Fork of the James River. December 29, 1767.

Anthony Kelley, 175 acres, Calfpasture River. April 2, 1768.

James Greenlee, 100 acres, South Side of the James River. Mentioned George Sulling. May 5, 1768.

James Arnold, 80 acres, South side of the James River. May 3, 1768.

Lily Brown, 250 acres, James River. April 26, 1768.

## Page 111

George Campbell, 76 acres, South side of James River. May 4, 1768.

Andrew Hays, 90 acres, North Branch of the James River. Adjoining Bordens patent. April 14, 1768.

John Fulton, 60 acres, Calfpasture River. April 3, 1768.

Patrick McConnel, 80 acres, Fork of the James River. Adjoining Bordens patent. March 25, 1768.

John Poage, Jr., 28 acres, Fork of the James River. Adjoining Samuel McClune. March 26, 1768.

Peter Wallace, 60 acres, Fork of the James River. Adjoining Bordens patent. April 11, 1768.

John Paxton, 60 acres, Fork of the James River. Adjoining Abram Browers. March 24, 1768.

James Templeton, 50 acres, Fork of the James River. Adjoining William Holman. March, 1768.

## Page 112

Christian Rhoads, 80 acres, South side of the James River. May 4, 1768.

John Meek, 48 acres, Calfpasture River. Mentioned Meeks, old line. April 3, 1768.

James Trimble, 145 acres, James River. October 26, 1767.

Malcom Allen, 310 acres, North side of the James River. April 25, 1768.

Nathaniel McClure, 150 acres, Forks of the James River. April 28, 1768.

Joseph Richison, 65 acres, Cowpasture River. Adjoining James Simpson. April 22, 1768.

Ann Miller, 50 acres, Cowpasture River. April 22, 1768.

## Page 113

William Gwynn, 185 acres, Bullpasture River. Adjoining Bond Estill. May 2, 1768.

Joseph Dennis, 200 acres, Forks of the James River. April 27, 1768.

Archibald Armstrong, 125 acres, Cowpasture. Adjoining John Rusk. April 4, 1768.

James Watson, 90 acres, Cowpasture. Adjoining James Lawrence. April 22, 1768.

Joseph Blaine, 80 acres, Cider Creek in the Forks of the James River. October 23, 1767.

Joseph Davis, 85 acres, Forks of the James River. April 11, 1768.

Samuel McCraken, 85 acres, Forks of the James River. Adjoining John and Alexander Walker. April 28, 1768.

## Page 114

Henry Waller, 75 acres, Branch of the James River. Adjoining James Simpson. April 22, 1768.

Richard Bodkin, 6 acres, Bullpasture River. Mentioned his mills. September 8, 1768.

Aurthur McClure, 43 acres, James River. Adjoining John Davis. November 24, 1768.

George Skillerin, 95 acres, Branch of Jackson River. Mentioned Wilson's Mill Creek. September 8, 1768.

William McKenney, 60 acres. Adjoining John Gilmore. July 7, 1768.

John Tate, 400 acres, Branch of Pine Run. Sept. 15, 1768.

Henry Cartmill, 25 acres, Purgatory Mountain, Forks of the James River. April 20, 1768.

John Davis, 50 acres, James River. Adjoining Aurthur McClure and his own land. November 24, 1768.

## Page 115

John Kelley, 110 acres, Calfpasture River. April 2, 1768.

John Walker, 140 acres, James River. Adjoining Buckhanan. May 30, 1768.

Edward Heins, 50 acres, Bullpasture River. Adjoining William Martin. September 8, 1768.

John Poage, 85 acres, Fork of the James River. Mentioned the Great Road. June 1, 1768.

James Logan, 80 acres, Fork of the James River. Adjoining John Gilmore and his own survey. July 7, 1768.

John Poage, 85 acres, Makey Run. Adjoining his own land. June 1, 1768.

Joshua Couts, 75 acres, Irish Creek. Adjoining Joseph Alexander. . . . . 16, 1768.

## Page 116

Robert Cambell, 140 acres, Head of Mary Creek. Adjoining Thomas Boyd, Samuel Steel, Robert McClanahan. September 29, 1768.

James Clency, 65 acres, Branch of the James River. December 1, 1768.

Samuel Forguson, 150 acres, Roanoke's Branch. November 28, 1768.

John Beard, 24 acres, Jennings Branch. May 10, 1768.

David Berry, 54 acres, East Branch of Muddy Creek. Adjoining Benjamin Kinley. November 24, 1768.

Edward Beard, 50 acres, North River of the Shenandoah. Adjoining David Leard, Joseph Dickinson, Hugh Donahoo. May 7, 1768.

David Bell, 152 acres, Fork of the South Branch of the Potomac. November 3, 1768.

## Page 117

John Brown, 73 acres, Linvils Creek. Adjoining Robert Patterson, John Gorden, and his own land. November 23, 1768.

Henry Ewin, 48 acres, Between the Branches of Cooks and Linvils Creek. Adjoining Jeremiah Harrison, (where he lives) and his own land. June 2, 1768.

Christopher Eye, 37 acres, Branch of the Blackthorn. November 8, 1768.

Michael Armoenst, 59 acres, South Branch of the Potomac. Adjoining John Gun. November 5, 1768.

John Chestnut, 10 acres, War Branch of a Branch of the North River. Adjoining William Chestnut, James Davison. June 4, 1768.

Reuben Daniel, 248 acres, Briery Branch of North River of the Shenandoah. Adjoining James Hanna. July 8, 1768.

Hugh Diver, 30 acres, North River of the Shenandoah. Adjoining Daniel Henderson. June 13, 1768.

## Page 118

John Gordon, 318 acres, Muddy Creek. Adjoining Thomas Shanklin, Archibald Hopkins, James Woods, and his own land. November 25, 1768.

James Hanna, 300 acres, Briery Branch. Adjoining James Diver and his own land. June 24, 1768.

John Weron, 285 acres, Cooks Creek. Adjoining Joseph Rutherford, Thomas Harrison. June 24, 1768.

Henry Leaborun, 273 acres, Jennings Branch. Adjoining William Chrestails. May 10, 1768.

Moses Hall, 213 acres, Mossey Creek. Adjoining Samuel McFeeters. October 11, 1768.

Jessee Haneson, 30 acres, Muddy Creek. Adjoining David Berry. November 24, 1768.

## Page 119

Mathias Leeher, 180 acres, Linvils Creek. Adjoining David Robinson and his own land. June 21, 1768.

Casper Miller, 164 acres, North River of the Shenandoah. Adjoining Jacob Pearisoner. May 5, 1768.

Samuel McFeeter, 180 acres, Mossey Creek, on Branch called the whet stone draft. June 15, 1768.

Elijah Garton, 154 acres, Dry River and Muddy Creek. Adjoining Bryan Muncey. November 26, 1768.

John Stepenson, 99 acres, Between Dry River and Beaver Creek. Adjoining Douglass. June 10, 1768.

Benjamin Kinley, 93 acres, Between Shanklin Gap and the white oak Bottom. June 7, 1768.

William Ralston, 110 acres, Mossey Creek. Adjoining Samuel McFeeters, and his own land. June 16, 1768.

## Page 120

John Botkin, 232 acres, Bullpasture River. Feb. 15, 1768.

Jacob Pearisioner, 250 acres, North River of the Shenandoah. Adjoining Grubbs. May 5, 1768.

Abraham Smith, 230 acres, Branch of Dry River of the Shenandoah. Adjoining Robert Henderson, John Davis. November 6, 1767.

John Jordan, 137 acres, Bullpasture. February 22, 1768.

Hugh Donoho, 116 acres, Frances Draft a Branch of Naked Creek. Adjoining Robert McCutchin, and his own land. March 7, 1768.

Charles Hays, 114 acres, Bullpasture Mountain. Adjoining Bill, John Jorden. November 15, 1768.

### Page 121

Benjamin Logan, 110 acres, on the North side of the North River of the Shenandoah, on the next small Branch below the mouth of Cooks Creek. December, 1767.

Margaret McGlaughlan, 110 acres, Dry River. Adjoining Charles Callachan, Stephenson. November 5, 1767.

Charles Smith, 76 acres, Forks of Potomac. Adjoining Davis, Dyer. November 4, 1767.

Thomas Miller, 227 acres, Fork South Branch of the Potomac. Mentioned Seneca River. October 30, 1767.

Alexander Miller, 45 acres, Branch of Cooks Creek. October 30, 1767.

Moses Thompson, 33 acres, Fork of the South Branch of the Potomac. October 28, 1767.

Henry Flesher, 50 acres, Fork of the South Branch of the Potomac. November 3, 1767.

### Page 122

Patrick Quin, 193 acres, South Side of Cooks Creek, a branch of the North River of the Shenandoah. Adjoining William Craven and his own land. Dec. 4, 1767.

Peter Venimon, 136 acres, Fork of the South Branch of the Potomac. Adjoining George Feeters. October 26, 1767.

Henry Lancescus, 45 acres, South Branch of the Potomac. October 31, 1767.

Jost Hinkle, 67 acres, South Branch of the Potomac. October 28, 1767.

Andrew Kinkade, 45 acres, Calfpasture River. Adjoining Finchers. February 13, 1768.

William Clifton, 98 acres, South Branch of the Potomac. Adjoining Thomas Willmot, Peter Venemon.

James Cunningham, 40 acres, South Branch of the Potomac. October 26, 1767.

Page 123

Benjamin Walker, 32 acres, South Branch of the Potomac. October 31, 1767.

Timothy Sweet, 32 acres, Fork of the Potomac. Adjoining Samuel Wilson. February 20, 1768.

Barnabas Mathews, 98 acres, Bullpasture River. February 22, 1768.

William Gibson, 53 acres, South branch of the Potomac. Mentioned one Scott. October 27, 1767.

Joseph Bennett, 40 acres, South Branch of the Potomac. October 27, 1767.

George Teter, 120 acres, South Branch of the Potomac. October 26, 1767.

Page 124

William McCellen, 96 acres, Bullpasture River. February 16, 1768.

Daniel Morris, 27 acres, Fork of the Potomac. Oct. 30, 1767

Godfrey Bumgardner, 26 acres, Fork of the Potomac. October 28, 1767.

Paul Teeter, 53 acres, Fork of the Potomac. Oct. 29, 1767.

Thomas Cambell, 54 acres West Fork of Cooks Creek. Mentioned Miller and his own line. December 2, 1767.

Robt. Duffell, 29 acres, Jordens Run, a Branch of Bullpasture River. February 16, 1767.

John Rion, 23 acres, Branch of the Potomac. Oct. 31, 1767.

Rosana Christian, 150 acres, Buffilo Creek Branch of Roanoke River. Adjoining Israel Christian. Aug. 5, 1767.

Page 125

Hugh Donaho, 231 acres, Naked Creek. Adjoining Gawan Leeper and his own line. March 7, 1768.

James Trotter, 133 acres, Small Branch of the North River of the Shenandoah. Adjoining James Henderson, (John) Grattan. April 11, 1768.

John Poage, 162 acres, South Branch of the Potomac. April 15, 1761.

William Heggons, 72 acres, on War Branch between Shanklins Gap and the White Oak Bottom. June 3, 1768.

Paulser Neighley, 68 acres, Small Branch of Crab Apple Bottom. November 5, 1768.

Henry Stone, 54 acres, Blackthorn. Mentioned Joseph Gamble. November 8, 1768.

Thomas Pickins, 22 acres, Linvils Creek. Adjoining Corne-
leus Reddles, June 22, 1768.

## Page 126

Jacob Gellesspey, 60 acres, Briery Branch. June 11, 1768.

Laurance Symmons, 26 acres, South Branch of the Potomac. Adjoining Gabral Gail. November 7, 1768.

John Slaven, 46 acres, On the waters of War Branch. June
3, 1768.

George Moffet, 604 acres, Middle River of the Shenandoah
Adjoining John Frances, William Anderson, John
Archer, John Young. Mentioned John Moffett patent.
March 14, 1767.

## Page 127

John Grattan, 1000 acres, North River of the Shenandoah.
Adjoining Hugh Campbell, John Hair. Jan. 19, 1769.

Michael Mallow, 72 acres, South Branch of the Potomac.
April 11, 1768.

Edward Erwin, 54 acres, Long Glade Branch of North
River. April 12, 1768.

John Burger, 50 acres, On Rockfish Gap Road. Mentioned
David Glen, Manus Burger and the Great Road. February 28, 1769.

John Stephenson, 65 acres, On same Drafts of Naked Creek,
beginning near a corner of his old tract. Jan. 31, 1769.

## Page 128

James Patterson, 344 acres, North Draft of Naked Creek.
Adjoining James Young, James Bell. Jan. 20, 1769.

James Young, 439 acres, Branch of Naked Creek. Adjoin-
ing James Patterson, James Bell, Edward Erwin,
James Dickeys. Mentioned Hugh Campbell, John
Young. February 16, 1769.

Samuel Steel, 238 acres, Shenandoah River. March 3, 1769.

Robert Reed, 190 acres, Middle River of the Shenandoah.
June 31, 1769.

## Page 129

Alexander Herron, 750 acres, West Branch of Cooks Creek,
498 acres, being part of a larger tract of land containing 1200 acres granted by patent to Robert McKay and
others the 26th day of March 1739 and then transfer-
red to Samuel Wilkins who at sundry times conveyed
the said 498 acres to the aforesaid Herron. Adjoining

Patrick Quin, (on the East side of Cooks Creek) Johnston, William Snowden, Trotter, Harrison. January 23, 1769.

William Snowden, 467 acres, West Fork of Cooks Creek. Adjoining Edward Shanklin. Mentioned John Wilkins and (Alexander) Herron. January 24, 1769.

Joshua Jack, 280 acres, South Mountain, on the head waters of Naked Creek. March 3, 1769.

Gutlip Eariff, 190 acres, Shenandoah River. Mentioned Fairfax boundery line. February 10, 1769.

Francis Kirkley, 110 acres, Naked Creek. March 4, 1769.

### Page 130

James Trimble, 400 acres, Calfpasture River. March 6, 1769.

Moses McClure, 400 acres. Adjoining Bordens patent and his own land. February 18, 1769.

William McMunay, 11 acres, James River. Adjoining his own former survey. February 22, 1769.

Samuel Walker, 110 acres, James River. Adjoining William McElahaney. February 13, 1769.

James Gilmore, 35 acres, Forks of the James River. Adjoining Moris Ofreals, Mary Ducharts, Dec. 13, 1768.

Patrick Caragan, 30 acres, James River. February 22, 1769.

Samuel Logue, 87 acres, Cowpasture. February 20, 1769.

### Page 131

Robert Alexander, 80 acres, Forks of the James River. Adjoining John Beaty. January 14, 1769.

David Wilson, 90 acres, Walker Creek. Adjoining William Thompson, Borden patent, and his own land. February 11, 1769.

William Thompson, 130 acres, Walker Creek. Adjoining James Mitchel, Elizabeth Bell, Kimsey. Feb. 8, 1769.

James Perry, 120 acres, Fork of the James River. February 13, 1769.

John Sympson, 92 acres, James River. Mentioned William McMunay. February 22, 1769.

Hugh Kelso, 45 acres, North Mountain. February 7, 1769.

Samuel Black, 65 acres. April 5, 1769.

### Page 132

Robert Jameson, 400 acres, Beverly Manor. Adjoining James Bell, Alexander Long. April 4, 1769.

Christopher Vineyard, 60 acres, James River. Adjoining·
John Bowyers. May 13, 1769.

James Kier, 250 acres, South Mountain. Adjoining Thomas
Steaurts. Mentioned Dewson Branch. April 4, 1769.

William McKee, 50 acres, House Mountain. Mentioned
David Qallace. May 1769.

Samuel Gibson, 98 acres, For kof the James River. May
19, 1769.

John and Alexander Walker, 180 acres, James River. May
31, 1769.

Joseph Long, 98 acres. May 18, 1769.

### Page 133

Halbert McClure, 150 acres, House Mountain of the waters
of Collens Creek. May 24, 1769.

James Trimble, 50 acres, Buffilo Creek Branch of James
Rriver. May 18, 1769.

John Summers, 98 acres, Fork of the James River. May 25,
1767.

Hugh Barkley, 95 acres, Fork of the James River. Adjoining McGavock, Robert Whitley. May 12, 1769.

Thomas Steaurt, 248 acres. April 4, 1769.

Samuel Davis, 85 acres, Buffilo Creek, Fork of the James
River. May 1769.

Robert McAnair, 83 acres, Fork of the James River. Adjoining David McCord. June 8, 1769.

### Page 134

William Preston, 250 acres, Branch of Little Catawba. February 25, 1769.

William Prestin, 256 acres, Catawba Creek, a Branch of the
James River. February 25, 1769.

John Buckhanan, 245 acres, James River. Adjoining Looneys. March 1, 1768.

Peter Dyerley, 62 acres, Roanoke River. Adjoining Alexander Love. May 25, 1768.

### Page 135

William Crow, 515 acres, James River. Adjoining Col.
Smith, Peter Looney, Joseph Looney. Sept. 2, 1767.

George Skilleren, 350 acres, Roanoke. Adjoining Daniel
McNeel, Armstrong. April 4, 1768.

John Mills, 230 acres, James River. March 3, 1768.

Thomas Stockton, 210 acres, Catawba Creek. Adjoining
David Mitchell. January 21, 1769.

James Alexander, 220 acres, Roanoke River. Feb. 2, 1768.

## Page 136

John Howard, 660 acres, Roanoke River. Adjoining Hugh Mills, Bouland. February 17, 1768.

Robert Brackinridge, 300 acres, Looneys Creek a Branch of the James River and Tinkers Creek a Branch of Roanoke River. Adjoining Edward Sharp, John Mills. February 20, 1768.

James Lauderdale, 280 acres, Looneys Creek. Feb. 24, 1768.

Alexander Evans, 185 acres, Back Creek a branch of the aJmes River. March 3, 1768.

## Page 137

James Rowland, 230 acres, Looneys Creek. Adjoining the Duth Cooper, Archibald Kyle. February 26, 1768.

Thomas Barnes, 165 acres, Roanoke River. Adjoining Campbells and his own land. September 11, 1767.

John Looney, 250 acres, Looneys Creek. March 4, 1768.

Andrew Harrison, 70 acres, Roanoke River. March 26, 1768.

John Looney, 196 acres, Looneys Creek. Adjoining John Mills, Mary Looney and his own patent. March 4, 1768.

Walter Stewart, 75 acres, Catawba. February 24, 1769.

## Page 138

John Eager, 140 acres, Roanoke River. Adjoining James Caghey. February 25, 1767.

Lemuel Andrews, 135 acres, Roanoke River. Adjoining John McClellon, William Faney, Jasper Faney, Thomas Foshes. May 29, 1767.

Isreal Christian, 205 acres, James River. March 4, 1768.

Francis Delaney, 96 acres, Roanoke River. Adjoining Cavins. February 19, 1768.

John Patterson, 50 acres, Patterson Creek Branch of the James River. February 11, 1768.

John Arthurs, 50 acres, Catawba Creek. Adjoining Fisher. March 15, 1768.

John Eager, 140 acres, Roanoke River. Adjoining James Caghey. February 25, 1767.

Lemuel Andrews, 135 acres, Roanoke River. Adjoining John McClellon, William Faney, Jasper Faney, Thomas Fashes. May 29, 1767.

Israel, Christian, 205 acres, James River. March 4, 1768.

Francis Delaney, 96 acres, Roanoke River. Adjoining Cavins. February 19, 1768.

John Patterson, 50 acres, Patterson Creek, Branch of the James River. Febuary 11, 1768.

John Arthurs, 50 acres, Catawba Creek. Adjoining Fisher. March 15, 1768.

## Page 139

Thomas Ferguson, 92 acres, Roanoke River. Feb. 3, 1768.

Hugh McNeil, 40 acres, James River. Adjoining McNeeley. February 27, 1768.

Isaiah Vansent, 65 acres, James River. Adjoining William Rawland. October 29, 1768.

John Charleton, 46 acres, Roanoke River. Adjoining Peter Dyerly. May 25, 1768.

Joseph Jenkins, 58 acres, James River. Adjoining Robert Breckinridge. February 2, 1768.

John Magee, 35 acres, Catawba Creek. Adjoining John Donelly. March 17, 1768.

Rebeca Bouland, 37 acres, Roanoke River. Adjoining John Bouland. February 18, 1768.

## Page 140

James McMillan, 50 acres, Catawba Creek. Adjoining John Donilley and his own land. March 18, 1768.

James Mellon, 53 acres, Roanoke River. Mentioned a Great Road. February 3, 1758.

Israel Christan, 240 acres, Roanoke River. Adjoining Mathew Emocks. February 18, 1769.

John Madison, 210 acres, Roanoke River. March 20, 1769.

John Madison, 75 acres, Roanoke River. Adjoining John Wilson. March 20, 1769.

Arthur Campbell, 320 acres, Catawba Creek. Oct. 12, 1769.

William Bryans, Jr., James Bryans, William Cowin and David Gass, 36 acres, Roanoke River. August 1, 1769.

James Barnet, 47 acres, Roanoke River. Adjoining James Robertson. November 11, 1767.

## Page 141

John Davidson, 170 acres, Collins Creek, branch of Shenandoah River. Adjoining Campbell. December 14, 1769.

Jacob Argenbright, 130 acres, Cub Run. Adjoining Jacob Nicholas. July 3, 1770.

Lewis Fridley, 145 acres, Stony Run, branch of Shenandoah River. July 4, 1770.

Augusteen Price, 73 acres, Peaked Mountain. Adjoining George Mallow. July 4, 1770.

Abraham Miller, 80 acres, Linville Creek. July 25, 1770.

Samuel Henphell, 125 acres, East Draft of Cooks Creek. Adjoining Harrison. November 15, 1770.

## Page 142

Andrew Bushong, 120 acres, Cub Run. Adjoining Robert William. Nov. 10, 1770.

Robert Dickey, 80 acres, Smiths Creek. Nov. 8, 1770.

John Ham, 295 acres, at a place called Flat Gap on both sides of the Great Road. Adjoining Boyers. November 7, 1770.

Robert Samples, 90 acres, Smiths Creek. Adjoining his own patent. October 29, 1770.

Felix Sheltman, 70 acres, Cooks Creek. Adjoining Thomas Harrison.

Edward Young, 80 acres, Cooks Creek. Adjoining (Samuel) Hemphell.

Thomas Pickett, 230 acres, South River of Shenandoah. December 12, 1770.

John Lewis, 80 acres, South Mountain, head of Elk Run, branch of the Shenandoah. December 19, 1770.

## Page 143

William Finley, 200 acres, South River of Shenandoah. Adjoining Robert Finley, Samuel Steel. March 2, 1769.

Alexander Miller, 175 acres, Cooks Creek. Adjoining Benjamin Harrison, Daniel Loves, William Bowyers and his own land. December 1, 1767.

Charles Teas, 98 acres, South side of South River of Shenandoah. Adjoining Thomas Turk and his own land. February 15, 1769.

John Black, 54 acres, South River of Shenandoah. February 17, 1769.

John Ramsey, 125 acres, South River of the Shenandoah. Mentioned Davis Gap Road. October 16, 1768.

Thomas Moore, 190 acres, Smiths Creek. Adjoining Michael Bowyer, Thomas Looker. May 5, 1769.

## Page 144

Daniel Grub, 88 acres, Smiths Creek. Adjoining Harman-

trout (Armentrout), Bell. May 25, 1769.
Daniel Smith, 200 acres, Smiths Creek. Adjoining James
    Wright. May 25, 1769.
Josiah Davison, 220 acres, Smiths Creek. July 13, 1770.
Henry Armantrout, 148 acres, Smiths Creek. Adjoining
    Valentine Smith. May 25, 1769.
Phillip Armantrout, 44 acres, Smiths Creek. May 26, 1769.
Robert Williams, 310 acres, Smiths Creek. Adjoining John
    Davis. May 26, 1769.
George Armantrout, 400 acres, Smiths Creek. Adjoining
    Daniel Grub. May 26, 1769.

### Page 145

Robert Craig. Adjoining Crawford. June 25, 1769. N. B.
    Charles Teas and John Craig sworn as chain carriers.
James Givens, 75 acres. Adjoining George Crawford, by
    the Great Road. June 25, 1769.
Adam Price, 135 acres, Cub Run. Adjoining John Craig.
    July 1, 1769. N. B. John Arganbright and Jacob Pence
    chain carriers.
William Herron, 225 acres between Cooks Creek and North
    River. Adjoining Snowden, McClure and his own land.
    January 24, 1769.
Phillip Harless, 400 acres. Adjoining Samuel Bell, Given,
    and his own patent. June 26, 1769.
Christian Clayman, 60 acres, South River of Shenandoah.
    Adjoining Trout and his own patent. Oct. 10, 1769.

### Page 146

Henry Liner, 90 acres, South River of Shenandoah. Adjoin-
    ing George Marten and Trout. Oct. 10, 1769.
Andrew Alexander, 194 acres, Back Creek, Branch of South
    River of Shenandoah. Mentioned Keenens line. March
    7, 1770.
James Craig, 235 acres, Middle River of Shenandoah. Ad-
    joining Denaho and his own patent. Nov. 24, 1769.
Brice Russell, 90 acres, Middle River of Shenandoah. Ad-
    joining Rankins, Donaho and his own patent. Nov. 25,
    1769.
William Campbell, 60 acres, Stony Lick Run a branch of
    North River of Shenandoah. Adjoining Matthew
    Thompson, Hook. December 5, 1769.
Thomas Beard, 80 acres, North River of Shenandoah. Ad-

joining Donaho. December 15, 1769.
Page 147
John Taylor, 230 acres, James River. Adjoining his own
land. August 3, 1769.
Caleb Worley, 400 acres, James River. August 8, 1769.
John Huston, 70 acres, Colliers Creek, Forks of James
River. Adjoining John Summers. August 3, 1769.
John Reed, 90 acres, James River. Adjoining George Bird-
wills. August 5, 1769.
John Summers, 130 acres, House Mountain, Fork of James
River. Adjoining Borden's patent. August 20, 1769.
Alexander Collier, 40 acres, Calfpasture River. September
13, 1769.
Page 148
John Dinwiddie, 115 acres, Jackson River. Mentioned Van-
derpools Gap, David Frames land. August 30, 1769.
Robert Dinwiddie, 98 acres, Vanderpools Gap. Sept. 1, 1769.
John Dunlap, 95 acres, Calfpasture River. Aug. 29, 1769.
Rev. John Brown, 70 acres, North Mountain. Sept. 13, 1769.
William Raigh, 125 acres, Calfpasture River. Adjoining
Alexander Crockett. Sept. 9, 1769.
John McCreery, 16 acres, Calfpasture River. Sept. 4, 1769.
Patrick McConnel, 170 acres, Calfpasture River. Sept. 11,
1769.
Uriah Humphrey, 45 acres, Calfpasture River. Adjoining
James Watson. February 23, 1769.
William McBride, 220 acres, Buffilo Creek Forks of James
River. August 24, 1769.
Page 149
James Morrow, 210 acres, branch of James River above
Vanderpool's Gap. Adjoniing Robert Dinwiddie. Sep-
tember 1, 1769.
James Raigh, 200 acres, Calfpasture River. Sept. 8, 1769.
Henry Gay, 80 acres, Calfpasture River. Sept. 11, 1769.
John Allison, 400 acres, Forks of James River. Adjoining
James Gilmer, crossing the Great Road. Sept. 28, 1769.
Thomas Beates, 85 acres, Buffalo Creek. Adjoining John
Long. October 14, 1769.
James Gilmer, 60 aocres, Forks of James River. Adjoining
Charles Allison, James Gilmer, September 27, 1769.
James Gilmerfi, 20 acres, Colliers Creek. Adjoining Patrick
McConnell and his old survey. October 13, 1769.

## Page 150

Andrew Alexander, 90 acres, Back Creek. Nov. 9, 1769.

Samuel Black, 400 acres, South River. Adjoining Beverley's patent, Henry Dawson, Edward Hall. Nov. 7, 1769.

James Bell, 320 acres. Adjoining Beverley and his own land. November 14, 1769.

James Bratton, 120 acres, between South River and Back Creek. Adjoining John King, Alexander Stuart. November 7, 1769.

William Callen, 280 acres. Adjoining Thomas Stuart, Henry Dawson, James Hars (or Heers). November 8, 1769.

James Cartmill, 90 acres, Purgatory Mountain. December 20, 1769.

Henry Dawson, 190 acres, South Mountain at Reid's Gap. November 10, 1769.

Henry Dawson, 340 acres, South River. Adjoining Thomas Stuart, Beverly Manor, November 8, 1769.

## Page 151

Soloman Turpine, 130 acres, Dry Fork, Smiths Creek. Adjoining Jeremaih Harrison and his own land. May 27, 1769.

Soloman Turpine, 220 acres, Linville Creek. Adjoining Walter Crow. May 27, 1769.

Jeremiah Harrison, 110 acres, Dry Fork of Smith's Creek. May 28, 1769.

Townsend Mathews, 400 acres, Dry fork of Smith's Creek. Adjoining Jeremiah Harrison, May 29, 1769.

Jacob Dickenson, 277 acres, Smiths Creek. Beginning at three pines on the East side of the Great Road, opposite to Reuben Harrison's land. May 30, 1769.

Reuben Harrison, 250 acres, Forks of Smith's Creek, beginning at two white oaks on the west side of a Great Road, on south side of John Ewins' land. May 30, 1769.

William Hinton, 100 acres, Smith's Creek. Adjoining John Ewins, Zebulon Harrison. May 30, 1769.

John Ray, 169 acres, Smith's Creek. Adjoining Reuben Harrison. May 30, 1769.

## Page 152

Zebulon Harrison, 84 acres, Smiths Creek. Adjoining John Harrison, Reuben Harrison. May 30, 1769.

John Needham, 144 acres, both sides of Smith's Creek below William Hinton. Adjoining Reuben Harrison, Zebulon Harrison. May 31, 1769.

Zebulon Harrison, 250 acres, East side of Smith's Creek. Adjoining John Needham and his own land. June 1, 1769.

Zebulon Harrison, 136 acres on east side of Smiths Creek. Adjoining Canols old tract, June 1, 1769.

John Alderson, 167 acres on east side of Smiths Creek. Adjoining his old tract. June 1, 1769.

Robert Dickey, 173 acres on east side of Smiths Creek. Adjoining Zebulon Harrison. June 1, 1769.

### Page 153

Thomas Looker, 165 acres on east side of Smiths Creek. Adjoining his old corner. June 1, 1769.

Thomas Loaker, 146 acres on east side of Smiths Creek. Mentioned Daniel James. June 1, 1769.

Abraham Smith, 82 acres, South Branch of the Potomac. Adjoining Cunningham, Gum. August 29, 1769.

George Eliot, 250 acres, Head Draft of the Fallin Spring. Beginning at three white oaks near a Great Road above Robert Young's land. September 14, 1769.

Thomas Moore, 250 acres, Smiths Creek. Adjoining Bowyers, Jacob Woodley, John Phililps. June 3, 1769.

Lewis Circle, 192 acres, on east side of Smiths Creek. Adjoining John Phillips, Thomas Moore. June 3, 1769.

Jacob Woodley, 35 acres on the east side of Smiths Creek. Adjoining his old corner. June 3, 1769.

### Page 154

Andrew Byrd, 270 acres, Between Mathew Harrisons and Millsaps lines. June 5, 1769.

Joseph Reice, 42 acres on west side of Smith Creek. Adjoining Andrew Byrd, Rambo. June 6, 1769.

Cornelius Riddle, 347 acres, east side of Linvils Creek. June 7, 1769.

David Robinson, 27 acres, North Fork of Shenandoah. Adjoining John Bear, Phillip Dealy, Isaac Robinson. June 8, 1769.

Conrad Webb, 120 acres, North Fork of Shenandoah. Adjoining Henry Brown. June 9, 1769.

Andrew Eweback, 81 acres, Head Branches of Holmans Creek. Adjoining Rowland. June 9, 1769.

Richard Rowland, 73 acres, Head Branches of Holmans Creek. Adjoining James Cunningham. June 9, 1769.

James Cunningham, 285 acres on the Head Branches of Holmans Creek. Adjoining Fairfax line, Richard Rowland. June 9, 1769.

## Page 155

John Bear, 616 acres, Branch of the North Shenandoah River. Adjoining Jacob Bear, Raders, Joel Robinson, Isaac Robinson. June 9, 1769.

Jacob Kaplinger, 52 acres, Branch of the North Shenandoah River. Adjoining his own land and Andrew Whitenlaugh. June 10, 1769.

Alexander Painter, 27 acres, Branch of the North Shenandoah River. Adjoining his own land, John Moore. June 10, 1769.

John Moore, 188 acres, Branch of North Shenandoah River. Adjoining his own land, Aron Hughs, Woods, Matthew Harrison. June 10, 1769.

Henry Brown, 150 acres, Branch of North Shenandoah River. Adjoining Michael Haber. Mentioned Hites Mines. June 12, 1769.

Joseph Thomas, 170 acres, Branch of North Shenandoah River. Adjoining Charles Lang, one Panninger. June 12, 1769.

## Page 156

John Whitmer, 239 acres, North branch of the Shenandoah. Adjoining Michael Haber. June 12, 1760.

Conrod Webb, 84 acres, North River of the Shenandoah. Adjoining George Mount, George Shoemaker, June 13, 1769.

Thomas Pickens, 143 acres, North River of the Shenandoah. Adjoining George Shoemaker. June 13, 1769.

James Sayers, 115 acres, Middle River of the Shenandoah. Adjoining James Trimble and his own land. June 30, 1769.

John Crawford, 312 acres, Briery Branch. Adjoining James Dever. August 23, 1769.

James Fowler, 650 acres, South Branch of the Potomac. August 25, 1769.

## Page 157

Michael Mallo, 114 acres, South Branch of the Potomac. August 26, 1769.

Joseph Skidmore, 19 acres, South Branch of the Potomac. August 26, 1769.

George Dyce, 240 acres, South Branch of the Potomac. Adjoining Evock August 27, 1769.

Francis and George Evock, 160 acres South Branch of the Potomac. Adjoining George Dyces. Aug. 27, 1769.

Barnet Lynch, 56 acres, Branch of Crab Apple Waters. Adjoining his old tract. August 29, 1769.

William West, 247 acres, Dry Fork of Smith Creek. Adjoining Townsend Mathew, Reuben Harrison. May 30, 1769.

John Poage, 150 acres, Cowpasture River. Adjoining John Bodkin, David Bell. December 8, 1769.

## Page 158

Patrick Lowry, 30 acres, North Branch of the James River. Adjoining his old survey. September 26, 1769.

William Laurence, 98 acres, Tams Creek Branch of the James River. February 23, 1769.

Samuel Laurence, Jr., 36 acres, James River. Dec. 8, 1769.

Alexander Long, 400 acres. Adjoining James Bell, William Long, Beverly. November , 1769.

William and John McKee, 50 acres, Forks of the James October 12, 1769.

John Moore, 50 acres, Lick Run, a Branch of Broad Creek. December 19, 1769.

Jacob Passinger, 310 acres, Cowpasture River. Mentioned William McMunay. December 4, 1769.

John Sterling, 30 acres, Forks of the James River. Adjoining Audley Paul, Henry Bown. Dec. 21, 1769.

## Page 159

Edward Green, 94 acres, Forks of the James River. Adjoining his own land Henry Cartmill, Maxwell. December 9, 1769.

Edward Green, 60 acres, Purgatory Mountain. Dec. 9, 1769

Robert Gillespey, 80 acres, Branch of the James River. December 7, 1769.

Robert Grey, 300 acres, South Mountain at Reeds Gap.

November 10, 1769.

Robert Hamilton, 98 acres, Branch of Back Creek. November 9, 1769.

Lazarus Inman, 200 acres, South River. Adjoining Isaac White, David Hendersin. November 11, 1769.

John King, 150 acres, Branch of Back Creek. Nov. 11, 1769

Patrick Kennon, 340 acres, branch of Back Creek, November 9, 1769.

## Page 160

James Sympson, 50 acres, Hanly Mill Creek. Branch of Cowpasture. December 20, 1769.

Moses Trimble, 150 acres, Head Springs of Buffilo Creek under Gump Mountain. Adjoining Andrew Smithers. May 18, 1767.

Isaac White, 94 acres, Back Creek and South River. Adjoining his old survey, John King. November 13, 1769

Arthur McClure, 96 acres, Forks of the James River. Adjoining his old survey. Devember 27, 1769.

Josiah East, 36 acres, North Branch of the James River. Adjoining Robinson. January 26, 1770.

Alexander Stuart, 340 acres, South River. Beginning at the mouth of Back Creek. Adjoinning John King, William Chesnut corner on the River bank called the Red Banks and his old survey. May 9, 1770.

## Page 161

Andrew Johnston, 353 acres, Muddy Creek. Mentioned Hends land. April 18, 1768.

Hugh Murphee, 542 acres, South Branch of the Potomac. December 14, 1769.

Valentine Metscaw, 130 acres, South Branch of the Potomac. December 15, 1769.

Hugh Green, 145 acres, Middle River of the Shenandoah. Adjoining Robert Stevenson, Thomas Stevenson, John Poage. December 29, 1769.

George Fultz, 67 acres, Branch of the South Mill Creek above little Walnut Bottom. December 15, 1769.

## Page 162

David Wilson Jr., 268 acres. Adjoining Samuel Gibson, Benjamin Logan. November 15, 1769.

Joseph Shreve, 200 acres, South Branch of the Potomac. December 13, 1769.

William Waterson, 173 acres, Middle River of the Shenandoah. Adjoining James Allen, Beverly Anderson, Rorbert Williams. November 4, 1769.

Martin Judy, 25 acres, South Branch of the Potomac.

William Cravens, 65 acres, Drafts of Cooks Creek. Adjoining his own land, William McGill, John Cravens, John Madison. November 16, 1769.

## Page 163

Henry Alford, 46 acres, Cooks Creek. Adjoining John Donald. November 14, 1769.

Frederick Havenor, 19 acres, South Fork of the Potomac. Adjoining his own land, Robert Davis. Dec. 18, 1769.

Jacob Friend, 20 acres, South Fork of the Potomac. December 11, 1769.

Alexander Miller, 90 acres, Drafts of Cooks Creek. Adjoining Daniel Loves, Daniel Harrison, William Bowyers, and his own land. May 5, 1770.

John Phillips, 136 acres, Middle River of the Shenandoah. Adjoining James Phillips. Mentioned his father's line. May 4, 1770.

Samuel McCleerey, 75 acres, Head Branches of Middle River of the Shenandoah. Adjoining Widow Patterson, James McCleery. May 3, 1770.

## Page 164

John Gum, 144 acres, branch of Crab Apple. Aug. 29, 1769

Samuel Cuney, 35 acres, Long Glade a Branch of the North River of the Shenandoah, Adjoining John Young, James Anderson, and his own land. May 12, 1770.

John Campbell, 250 acres, Draft Middle River. Adjoining Alexander Walker. March 28, 1770.

Alexander McKenny, 310 acres, Middle River. Adjoining David Stuarts, Phillips, John McKenny. March 14, 1770.

John Britt, 77 acres, Middle River. Adjoining Jacob Campbell, James Craig, March 28, 1770.

Samuel Craig, 26 acres, Branch of McClures Run a Branch of Middle River. March 16, 1770.

## Page 165

John Taylor, 190 acres, Spring Draft a Branch of Cub Run. November 28, 1769.

Robert Eliot, 33 acres, Cub Run a Branch of Shenandoah. Adjoining William Beard. November 28, 1769.

Jacob Hornberry, 65 acres, North River of the Shenandoah Mentioned Funks Hill. December 15, 1769.

James Belshie, 220 acres, Branch of the North River of the Shenandoah. Adjoining Robert Belshie, and his own land. December 15, 1769.

Archibald Huston, 80 acres, North side of his patent. December 16, 1769.

Thomas Dooley, 315 acres, On South Mountain near the great road. March 16, 1770.

Charles Neil, 98 acres, North River. Adjoining Donaho, ember 15, 1769.

Jacob Peters, 50 acres, on Peters Spring Branch, a branch of Elk Run. March 13, 1770.

## Page 166

Francis Kirkley, 225 acres, South Fork of Naked Creek at a a place called the Grape Thicket Ridge  on the  South Mountain. March 13, 1770.

Francis Kirkley and Reuben Roach, 150 acres, on top of South Mountain. Adjoining Joshua Rush.  March 14, 1770.

Francis Meadow, 80 acres, North Fork of  the  Hawksbill. March 15, 1770.

Cornelius White, 150 acres, North Fork of the Hawksbill. Adjoining Meadow. March 16, 1770.

John Davis, 50 acres,  on top South Mountain.  March 17, 1770.

Jacob Boughman, 115 acres, Hawksbill. March 17, 1770.

Valentine Cook, 170 acres, Hawksbill. March 17, 1770.

## Page 167

Robert Shanklin, 1000 acres, Between the North River of the Shenandoah and Mill Creek, including 150 acres old patent granted to the said Shanklin on  the  12th  of May 1759. Adjoining Deniston. December 6, 1769.

Henry and John Perkey, 1000 acres, Mill Creek, a branch of North River of the Shenandoah, including 350 acres granted to by patent to William Williams, the 30 days of June 1743, and one other tract of  land  containing 200 acres granted to Jacob Stover by patent dated the 13th of December 1788; which lands afterwards became vested in Henry Perkey deceased, who devised the same to the aforesaid Henry and John Perkey. Adjoining William Hook, Shanklin. March 2, 1770.

John Monger, 84 acres, North side of the Shenandoah River. Adjoining Francis Kerkley and his own land. April 30, 1770.

## Page 168

John Hedrick, 90 acres, North Side of the Shenandoah River. Adjoining his own land, Jacob Mann, Teeter, Seller. April 19, 1770.

Michael Shirley, 90 acres, Between the Peaked Mountain and the Shenandoah. Adjoining John Sellers, Green Grant. April 19, 1770.

Samuel Thornhill, 145 acres, Between the Peaked Mountain and the Shenandoah River. Adjoining Kersh. April 20, 1770.

George and Stephen Conrad, 105 acres, Between the Peaked Mountain and the Shenandoah River. Adjoining Samuel Thornhill, Fulch, John Monger, John Seller. April 20, 1770.

John Lingle, 300 acres, Quails Run Branch of the Shenandoah. Adjoining Huffman. April 21, 1770.

Jacob Runkle, 33 acres, Stoney Run Branch of the Shenandoah. Adjoining Treslers, and his own patent. April 23, 1770.

John Herdman, 30 acres, Branch of Boons Run a Branch of the Shenandoah. Adjoining Huffman. April 23, 1770.

John Fulch, 40 acres, North side of the Shenandoah. Adjoining John Monger and his own land. April 24, 1770.

## Page 169

Mathias Keish, 180 acres, Between the Peaked Mountain and the Shenandoah. Adjoining Sellers and his own land. November 24, 1770.

Christian Miller, 190 acres, Elk Run a Branch of the Shenandoah. Adjoining Magot, Henry Miller, Smith. April 24, 1770.

Peter and Phillip Conrad, 130 acres, Elk Run Branch of the Shenandoah. April 27, 1770.

Henry Miller, 390 acres, on the Shenandoah. Adjoining his patent. April 28, 1770.

Jacob Bear, 345 acres, On the Shenandoah. Adjoining his

62          ABSTRACT OF SURVEYS

patent. April 28, 1770.
Abraham Miller, 200 acres, South side of the Shenandoah. Adjoining Jacob Bear. April 28, 1770.
Peter Assum, 110 acres, Between the Peaked Mountain and the Shenandoah. Adjoining  Daniel Sink,  Prunemer, Peter Fisher. April 30, 1770.

Page 170

James Bryson, 380 acres, on the South Mountain, on the Head Waters of the Hawksbill. May 1, 1770.
Phillip Lingle, 310 acres, Between the Shenandoah and the Mountain. Adjoining James Fraizer, Thomas Lewis, Miller, Crossing a Road. May 12, 1770.
Jacob Miller, 550 acres, Between Shenandoah and the South Mountain.  Adjoining James Frazier. Thomas Lewis Crossing a Road. May 12, 1770.
Joachim Van Farson, (The Dutch Lord), 1000 acres, Between the Branches of Cooks Creek, Smiths Creek, and Cub Run. April 25, 1770.

Page 171

William Chestnut, 320 acres, South River,  Beginning at Red Bank, corner to Alexander Stuart, Beverly Manor. May 8, 1770.
James Bell, 220 acres. South River.  Adjoining Alexander Long, and his own land. May 5, 1770.
John Wilkinson, 800 acres of land inclusive of two tracts containing 400 acres each, lying between Beverly Manor and the South Mountain.  Adjoining Lazarus Jarman, John Campbell, William Teas. May 9, 1776.
John Wilkinson, 800 acres, Between the South River  and South Mountain near Rockfish Gap. Adjoining William Teas, Samuel Steel, Finley. May 10, 1770.

Page 172

John Wilkeson, 780 acres, between South River and South Mountain.  Adjoining  Edward  Hall,  King,  Stuart, Chestnut. May 7, 1770.
John Wilkison, 400 acres, joining the lines of Beverly Manor, William Chestnut. May 7, 1770.
Lewerence Bell, 105 acres, Between Smiths Creek and the Mountain.  Adjoining his patent. November 8, 1770.
Mathias McGlammery, 590 acres, Smith Creek. Adjoining Harrison, Needham. November 2, 1770.

## Page 173

Thomas Harrison, 1290 acres, On East Draft of Cooks Creek, including 233, acres granted to him by patent dated March 15th, 1744. Adjoining Sheltman, Black. November 13, 1770.

John Sheltman, 85 acres, On a Branch of Cooks Creek. Adjoining his own patent. November 12, 1770.

Reuben Harrison, 194 acres, West side of Smiths Creek. October 30, 1770.

Joseph Goare, 290 acres, West side of Smiths Creek. October 31, 1770.

## Page 174

Thomas Alderson, 80 acres, adjoining Jacob Woodley, Looker, Carols, November 2, 1770.

Thomas Looker, 90 acres, Smiths Creek. Adjoining Bowyer. October 3, 1770.

Thomas Looker, 165 acres, Smiths Creek. Adjoining Woodley, Muney. November 9, 1770.

Jacob Woodley, 150 acres, Smiths Creek. Adjoining Looker. November 2, 1770.

John Peartree, 200 acres, Smiths Creek. Adjoining Woodly; Goare. November 3, 1770.

## Page 175

Robert Armstrong, 583 acres, Jennings Branch. Adjoining John Kirk, Robert McCetterick. April 17, 1770.

Alexander Walker, 159 acres, Middle Branch of Shenandoah. Adjoining Thomas Cornely. March 28, 1770.

James Bell, 85 acres, Middle Branch of Shenandoah. Adjoining James Phillips. May 30, 1770.

Andrew McClure, 66 acres, Middle Branch of Shenandoah. Adjoining Beverlys, William Mathus. March 8, 1770.

John Burnside, 21 acres, Middle Branch of Shenandoah Adjoining Cohorn, Thomas Stevenson. March 9, 1770.

William Armstrong, 14 acres, Middle Branch of Shenandoah. March 17, 1770.

## Page 176

Sampson and George Mathews, Calfpasture River, 1200 acres granted to William Beverley, also 400 acres and 480 acres. April 5, 1770.

Henry Waterson, 100 acres, Middle River. Adjoining Morris Ofreal. March 15, 1770.

Thomas Moore, 300 acres, Smiths Creek. Adjoining Michael Bowyers, John Phillips. June 3, 1770.

John Poage, 268 acres, branch of Middle River. Adjoining James Allen, Hugh Green. Mentioned Robert Reed and Great Road. October 26, 1770.

John Stuart, 45 acres, Middle River. Adjoining Sam Hend, Tim Colls. October 17, 1770.

### Page 177

Robert Hamilton, 130 acres, Back Creek, branch of Shenandoah. Adjoining Alexander. March 7, 1770.

William Givens, 329 acres, Jackson River. Adjoining Ralph Lafarty. Mentioned Thomas Lewis. October 5, 1770.

George Crawford, 194 acres, Middle River. Adjoining Samuel Henderson, Alexander Walker. June 26, 1770.

Steven Willson, 350 acres, Jackson River. October 5, 1770.

John Kindkead, 54 acres, Calfpasture River. Aug. 17, 1770.

### Page 178

Samuel Henderson, 117 acres, Middle River. Adjoining James Givens, William Johnson. June 26, 1770.

William Stuart, 65 acres, Cowpasture River. Adjoining James Botkins. October 6, 1770.

John Alleson, 64 acres, Middle River. Adjoining Andrew McClure, Beverley Manor. October 17, 1770.

David Lowderback, 164 acres, Shenandoah River. Adjoining John Fultz near Fairfaxes line. June 15, 1770.

John Needham, 60 acres, Smiths Creek. October 20, 1770.

John Ray, 65 acres, Smiths Creek. Adjoining Harrison, Ewin, and his survey. October 30, 1770.

### Page 179

Richard Ragan, 170 acres, Head of the East Draft of Cooks Creek. Adjoining John Haneson, Sheltman, and his own patent. June 15, 1771.

Henry Sellers, 95 acres, Shenandoah River. Adjoining Sherley and his own land. June 18, 1771.

Christain Teeter, 85 acres, branch of Shenandoah River. January 20, 1771.

John Couts, 80 acres, branch of Shenandoah River. Adjoining Teeters. January 20, 1771.

Jacob Herman, 70 acres, branch of Shenandoah River. Adjoining Couts. January 2, 1771.

James Moniee, 140 acres, Elks Run in the South Mountain. Adjoining Thomas Dooley. March 5, 1771.

### Page 180

Martin Gryton, 80 acres, Smiths Creek. Adjoining John Davis Decd, Armentrout, Thomas Harrison. May 1, 1771.

Martin Gryton, 248 acres, Smiths Creek. Adjoining John Davis Decd., Thomas Harrison, Reuben Harrison, May 1, 1771.

Cornelius Hily, 200 acres, Smiths Creek. May 2, 1771.

George Armentrout, 85 acres, Smiths Creek. Adjoining Bells. May 1, 1771.

John Alderson, 26 acres, Smiths Creek. Adjoining his own land, May 2, 1771.

Zebulon Harrison, 110 acres, Smiths Creek. Adjoining his own patent. May 2, 1771.

Conrad Smith, 30 acres, Dry Fork of Smiths Creek. Adjoining John Ewins, John Ray, May 3, 1771.

Jonathan Hilyard, 235 acres, between Smiths Creek and the Long Meadows. May 3, 1771.

Anthony Ailor (Eiler), 45 acres, Peaked Mountain. Adjoining Nicholas. May 4, 1771.

### Page 181

John Cummins, 98 acres, Mary Creek. Adjoining William Alexander, James Ritchey, John Lusk, Bordens. December 8, 1770.

Arthur Graham, 40 acres, Bordens Patent. Feb. 14, 1771.

Michael Coulter, 80 acres, North Mountain. Adjoining Bordens. February 15, 1771.

John Thompson, 28 acres, Cars Creek. Adjoining the heirs of Thomas Gilmore, Decd. November 30, 1770.

Jacob Nicholas, 460 acres, Cub Run, including 390 acres being part of a Great tract of 3000 acres which Christopher Francisco purchased of Jacob Stover and still is a part of a greater tract of 5000 acres granted by patent under the seal of the Colony to the said Stover. Adjoining Argenbright, Passinger, Hetrick. May 11, 1771.

### Page 182

William Blayer, (Blair) 132 acres, branch of Naked Creek. Adjoining John Stephenson. January 27, 1771.

Abraham Smith, 317 acres, Dry River in a Gap of North

66 ABSTRACT OF SURVEYS

Mountain. December 21, 1770.
John McVay, 238 acres, North River of Shenandoah. Adjoining David Williams. March 7, 1771.
John Thomas, 300 acres, Brocks Creek including a survey of 140 acres first granted to Reece Thomas by patent dated the 16th of August, 1756. Adjoining Bordens, Haverstick. December 28, 1770.
Thomas Waddle, 25 acres, North River of Shenandoah. Adjoining Robert Edgar, Lampler. March 6, 1771.

Page 183
Joseph Rheaburn, 122 acres, Middle River. Adjoining Robert Reed, Hugh Green, Robert Stephenson. January 3, 1771.
Joseph Rheaburn, 238 acres, Mossey Creek called Pudding Spring. March 5, 1771.
Samuel Erwin, 111 acres, Middle River. Adjoining Jane Erwin, Frances Corner, Robert Stephenson. January 5, 1771.
Isaac Robinson, 71 acres, North River of Shenandoah. Adjoining John Bear and his own land. Jan. 8, 1769.
John Rice, 199 acres, Briery Branch in the Gap of North Mountain. December 19, 1770.
Thomas Huston, 279 acres, Western Branches of Linvils Creek. December 24, 1770.

Page 184
Reece Thomas, 433 acres, Head Brocks Creek, first granted to Cornelius Cook. December 28, 1770.
Francis Green, 198 acres Linvils Creek. Adjoining James Calhoon and his old tract. December 24, 1770.
Joseph Brown, 20 acres. Adjoining Thomas Douglas, Nicholas Mace. December 24, 1770.
Robert McKetbreck, 100 acres, Jennings Branch. Adjoining Samuel Morras, Charles Floyds, John Poage. Mentioned Henry Marra. July 16, 1771.
Alexander Kilpatrick, 120 acres, branch of Middle River. Including a tract of 90 acres granted to William Cunningham by patent dated February 12, 1755, and was conveyed by Charles Kilpatrick, Decd. July 7, 1771.

Page 185
James Trimble, 550 acres, Middle River. Adjoining James Layer. July 17, 1771.

William Christall, 290 acres, Jennings Branch. Adjoining Mathew Edmiston, Thomas Beard. July 16, 1771.

William McCamey, 280 acres, branch of North River of Shenandoah. Adjoining Roger Kilpatrick. July 6, 1771.

John Hogshead, 200 acres, Jennings Branch. Adjoining Robert McKellerick, Samuel Morras. July 16, 1771.

Page 186

Joseph Lindon, 90 acres, Middle River. Adjoining Alexander Walker, Thomas Rankin. November 5, 1771.

Michael Warren, 400 acres. Adjoining another tract of his land, and Jacob Warren. September 20, 1771.

Timothy Warren, 85 acres, branch of Linvils Creek. Adjoining Felix Gilbert, Francis Green, Daniel Harrison. September 21, 1771.

Jean Reabrean, 96 acres, North River of Shenandoah. Adjoining Joseph Lindon, Thomas McMahon, Jacob Campbell, Thomas Rankin. November 6, 1771.

Thomas Bryant, 54 acres, Linvils Creek. Adjoining Jawl Gum, Cornelius Bryant. September 19, 1771.

John Brown, 28 acres, branch of Linvils Creek. Adjoining his own land. September 23, 1771.

Andrew Euine, 13 acres, Drafts of Linvils Creek. Adjoining Robert Patterson. September 23, 1771.

Page 187

David Frame, 194 acres, Jacksons River. Adjoining William Myas, Francis Frame. July 22, 1771.

Robert Dinwiddie, 97 acres, Jacksons River. Adjoining his own land and William Myas. July 20, 1771.

Patrick Miller, 45 acres, Cowpasture River. Adjoining. William Black and his own land. July 25, 1771.

Henry Gay, 98 acres, Cowpasture River. Adjoining Andrew Donely and his old survey. Decmber 1769.

Robert Hamilton, 185 acres, Back Creek. Adjoining John Wilkerson. November 18, 1771.

James Braden, 300 acres, Back Creek. November 21, 1771.

William Long, 90 acres, Back Creek. Adjoining Alexander Long. November 26, 1771.

Page 188

Denes Manis, 400 acres. Adjoining Wilkerson, Hamilton. November 18, 1771.

68	ABSTRACT OF SURVEYS

Robert Grey, 70 acres, Back Creek. November 22, 1771.
Robert Grey, 150 acres, Back Creek. Adjoining Samuel
Woods. November 21, 1771.
James Kerr, 400 acres. Adjoining his old survey, Thomas
Stuarts, Samuel Black. November 25, 1771.
David Caldwell, 400 acres, Back Creek. Adjoining his old
survey, Robert Hamilton. November 23, 1771.
Thomas and Samuel Willson, 63 acres. Adjoining their own
land. November 28, 1771.
John Weaver, 280 acres, between South Mountain and
South River. November 28, 1771.

Page 189
Hugh McCaury, 400 acres, between South River and the
Mountain. Adjoining James Kerrs, William Collins,
Johnathan Waters. November 20, 1771.
John Caldwell, 350 acres. Adjoining William Long, Alexan-
der Long. November 27, 1771.
Hugh Means, 170 acres, Horse Run a branch of Pine Run.
Mentioned Great Road. November 27, 1771.
Jonathan Waters, 200 acres, Cold Run branch of South
River. Adjoining William Collins. November 23, 1771.
Run the division line between Augusta and Botetourt.
Fees for running four and three quarters miles, 1000 pence.
Fees for running twenty-three and a half miles, 1675 pence.
Settlement with the Colledge in April, 1772 . . . . . .

Page 190
Thomas Deverik, 135 acres, Cowpasture River. Adjoining
Alexander Miller. December 31, 1771.
Thomas Willmott, Jr.., 38 acres, Potomac River. December
3, 1771.
Ludwrick Wagoner, 131 acres, Potomac River.
Francis Green, 173 acres, branch of Linvils Creek. Adjoin-
ing Even Thomas. September 19, 1771.
John Skidmore, 170 acres, branch of South Potomac River.
December 12, 1771.
William Cunningham, 83 acres, branch of South Potomac
River. December 14, 1771.
Frederick Glassprenard, 83 acres, branch South Potomac
River. December 1771.
Christopher Lick, 17 acres, branch of South Potomac River,
December 23, 1771.

## Page 191

John Skidmore, 237 acres, South Branch Potomac. December 7, 1771.

Michael Proops, 72 acres, South Branch Potomac.

William Cunningham, 150 acres, South Branch Potomac. December 13, 1771.

Phillip Teeter, 118 acres, South Branch Potomac. Adjoining Ab. Hinkle. December 17, 1771.

John Bennet, 135 acres, South Branch Potomac. Dec. 10, 1771.

James Dyerly, 104 acres, South Branch Potomac. December 27, 1771.

Michael Wiltfong, 50 acres, South Branch Potomac.

Thomas Willmot, 61 acres, South Branch Potomac. December 2, 1771.

## Page 192

Moses Elsworth, 357 acres, South Branch Potomac River. December 18, 1771.

George Hurst, 61 acres, South Branch Potomac River. December 21, 1771.

John Blizzard, 28 acres, South Branch Potomac River. December 26, 1771.

David Reel, 110 acres, South Branch Potomac River. Adjoining Henry Bopart. December 21, 1771.

Christian Yeasell, 39 acres, South Branch Potomac River. Adjoining Fairfax line. December 24, 1771.

Frederick Cape, 39 acres, South Branch Potomac River. December 21, 1771.

George Waldrum, 68 acres, South Branch Potomac River. December 19, 1771.

Henry Bopart, 52 acres, South Branch Potomac River. Adjoining Jacob Peters. December 20, 1771.

## Page 193

Moses Thompson, 133 acres, South Fork Potomac. December 9, 1771.

David Harmon, 125 acres, South Fork Potomac. December 14, 1771.

Godfrey Bumgardner, 127 acres, South Fork Potomac. December 14, 1771.

James Cunningham, 98 acres, South Fork Potomac. December 13, 1771.

Jacob Moats, 53 acres, South Fork Potomac. Adjoining James Dyer. December 27, 1771.

William Smith, 52 acres, South Fork Potomac. December 12, 1771.

Jacob Ham, South Fork Potomac, December 9, 1771.

Jacob Springstone, 91 acres, South Fork Potomac. December 12, 1771.

## Page 194

Jacob Elsworth, 215 acres, South Fork Potomac. December 18, 1771.

David Mathews, 184 acres, South Fork Potomac. December 17, 1771.

Abraham Smith, 115 acres, South Fork Potomac. December 11, 1771.

John Nelson, 90 acres, South Fork Potomac. Adjoining David Harmons. December 17, 1771.

Andrew Fule, 81 acres, South Fork Potomac. Mentioned Henry Pickle. December 30, 1771.

Michael Baush, 53 acres, South Fork Potomac. Mentioned Fairfax line. December 21, 1771.

Peter Smith, 65 acres, South Fork Potomac. Adjoining George Simmons and his own land. December 31, 1771.

Thomas Summerville, 33 acres, South Fork Potomac. December 3, 1771.

## Page 195

James Cuney, 350 acres, South Fork of Linvils Creek, including a tract of 245 acres first granted to Samuel Harrison by patent and conveyed to William Minter. Adjoining Walter Crow, and his own land. September 21, 1771.

Arthur Connely, 530 acres, branch of Middle River. Adjoining John Campbell, George Crawford, Samuel Henderson, Patrick Crawford, Colman, William Johnston. January 9, 1772.

Robert Curry, 400 acres, between the Glade and Mossey Creek. September 9, 1771.

George Finley, 35 acres, Middle River. Adjoining Edward Bradin, William Anderson. January 25, 1772.

Peter Venomon, 150 acres, South Branch Potomac. Adjoining Joseph Skidmore. December 11, 1771.

John Finley, 97 acres, branch of Middle River. Adjoining William Henderson and his own land. Jan. 25, 1772.

Hugh Donohue, 195 acres, Naked Creek. Adjoining Robert McCuschin and his own land. January 9, 1772.

## Page 196

John Poage, 550 acres, South Branch of Potomac. Adjoining Shelton. May 5, 1772.

Peter Kole, 90 acres, South Branch of Potomac. Adjoining Michael Mallows, Shelton. May 5, 1772.

Christian Wagoner, 89 acres, South Branch of Potomac. April 7, 1772.

Henry Stone, 69 acres, South Branch of Potomac. March 30, 1772.

Nicholas Harper, 36 acres, South Branch of Potomac. March 31, 1772.

Christopher Eye, 35 acres, South Branch of Potomac. March 27, 1772.

James Diver, 126 acres, Bever Creek. Adjoining Daniel Henderson. March 25, 1772.

Bastain Hover, 89 acres, South Branch of Potomac. Adjoining Henry Stone, Mark Swadley. March 28, 1772.

## Page 197

Abraham Smith, 350 acres, Bever Creek. Adjoining Hugh Diver, Daniel Henderson. March 25, 1772.

Joseph Douglass, 400 acres, North River of Shenandoah. Adjoining Abraham Smith, Hugh Douglass. March 26, 1772.

George Somvalt, 236 acres, South Branch of Potomac. March 31, 1772.

Michael Armocust, 98 acres, South Branch of Potomac. Adjoining Barnet Lance. April 7, 1772.

Barnet Lance, 50 acres, South Branch Potomac. Adjoining Abraham Smith, Michael Armocust. April 8, 1772.

Peter Sickenfoot, 250 acres, South Branch Potomac. Adjoining Adam Harper. April 8, 1772.

John Young, 94 acres, South Branch Potomac. Adjoining Peter Hoal, April 8, 1772.

Christian Neigley, 118 acres, South Branch Potomac. Adjoining Peter Sickenfoot. April 8, 1772.

## Page 198

Peter Hoal, 97 acres, branch of Jackson River. April 10, 1772.

George Nicholas, 130 acres, South Branch Potomac, April 10, 1772.

Peter Flesher, 93 acres, South Branch Potomac. Adjoining Nicholas Harper.

James Wood, 130 acres, South Branch Potomac. Adjoining Joseph Gambel. April 12, 1772.

Peter Venomen, 148 acres, South Branch Potomac. Adjoining Valentine Castel. December 4, 1771.

John Poage, 200 acres, Jennings Gap in North Mountain. Adjoining Robert McKetbrick. June 16, 1772.

James Gamble, 200 acres, Head Branch of Naked Creek. Adjoining William Frame and his own land. June 14, 1772.

## Page 199

James Hogshead, Jr., 379 acres, branch of Middle River. Mentioned Robert Rolston. August 26, 1772.

John Seawright, 102 acres, Naked Creek. Adjoining Hugh Donohue, John King. Mentioned Joseph Stover. July 2, 1772.

Moses Thompson, 133 acres, South Branch Potomac. July 27, 1772.

John Madison, Jr., 500 acres, East Fork of Cooks Creek, including 141 acres part of a tract of 200 acres granted to Robert Cravens by patent dated Feb. 10, 1748; and 200 acres adjoining the same granted to John Madison, Sr., by patent dated July 10, 1766. Which several pieces of land became vested in John Madison, Jr. Adjoining John Cravens, Joseph Cravens. July 18, 1772.

## Page 200

Jacob Bear, 72 acres, Shenandoah River. Mentioned David Frazer, the Great Road. June 5, 1772.

Peter Miller, 95 acres, branch of Cub Run. Adjoining Robert Williams, James Laird. June 23, 1772.

Samuel Rolston, 168 acres, Mossey Creek. Adjoining John McCoy, William Rolston. July 17, 1772.

Daniel Price, 85 acres, Peaked Mountain. Adjoining Henry Julius, Henry Lung. July 27, 1772.

David Sink, 43 acres, Shenandoah River. Adjoining Huffman and his own land. July 27, 1772.

John Davis, 153 acres, branch of Jackson River. Adjoining William Cunningham. October 10, 1772.

John Baxter, 124 acres, Jackson River. October 9, 1772.

William Gregory, 104 acres, Jackson River. Adjoining William Cunningham. October 10, 1772.

Page 201

Thomas Turk, 300 acres. Adjoining Keneleys and his own land. June, 1772.

John Dickson, 165 acres, Middle River. Adjoining John Allesan, Andrew McClure, John Stuart. Oct. 31, 1772.

John McClure, 300 acres, North River. Adjoining Hugh Duglass, John Logan, John McGill, William Herron, Morris. Mentioned that the line runs to the mouth of Dry River. July 14, 1772.

Thomas Bryant, 350 acres, Head Branch of Long Meadow, a branch of the North Fork of Shenandoah. Adjoining Mathias Leacher. July 17, 1772.

James Willson, 90 acres, North Mountain. Adjoining William Crawford. July 17, 1772.

William Allison, 31 acres, Middle River. Adjoining James Kerr and his own land. July 9, 1772.

Page 202

John Skidmore, 63 acres, South Branch of Potomac. Adjoining Jacob Conrad.

Adam Lough, 53 acres, South Branch of Potomac. Adjoining Adam Harpools and his own land. Oct. 14, 1772.

William McClure, 48 acres, Middle River. Adjoining Hugh Allen, John Cockran. October 18, 1772.

Samuel Vanee, 47 acres, Jackson River. October 9, 1772.

John Davis, 43 acres, Jackson River. Adjoining William Hutcheson. October 10, 1772.

John Parks, 292 acres, Mary Creek, branch of James River. Adjoining William Chambers, Keys. October 12, 1772.

Robert Sraw, 37 acres, Mary Creek, branch of James River. October 21, 1772.

Page 203

James McClung, 43 acres, Mary Creek, branch of James River. October 22, 1772.

Robert Weir, 49 acres. Adjoining Thomas Boyd, John Boyd. October 23, 1772.

Hugh Tarbut, 400 acres, South River. Adjoining William Camble, Beverley patent. October 24, 1772.

John Caldwell, 552 acres, South River. October 28, 1772.

William McGavock, 75 acres, Irish Creek on a ridge of the
South Mountains called the Dutch Pond Ridge. July 2,
1772.
Page 204
Alexander Walker, 70 acres, Walkers Creek. Adjoining
Hugh Kelso, Burdens patent, Anthony Kelly. July 28,
1772.
John Wilson, 50 acres, Walkers Creek and on the N. E.
end of the Jump Mountain. July 28, 1772.
John Lyle, 16 acres, Irish Creek. July 3, 1772.
James Mitchel, 144 acres, Middle River. Adjoining Samuel
Hay, James Moffet, William Campbell, Robert Jame-
son. July 21, 1771.
Page 205
James Greenlee, 408 acres, (It being part of a tract of land
containg 92,100 acres granted to Benjamin Burdin by
patent the 6th November, 1739) which became the pro-
perty of Jacob Grey and by ajudgement of the Gener-
al Court on ye 27th of October, 1772 for non-payment
of quitrents, was adjudged to the said Greenlee. Ad-
joining Rev. John Brown, John Huston. April 27, 1773.
Adam Sellers, 542 acres, Shenandoah River. Adjoining
John Miller, Samuel Thornhill, Mathias Scarce, Henry
Sellers, Peter Sellers.
Peter Sellers, 183 acres, Shenandoah River. Adjoining
Christian Teeter, Adam Sellers. March 4, 1773.
Page 206
Thomas Poage, 50 acres, being part of a large tract of
land called Beverley Manor containg 118,491 acres,
formerly granted to William Beverley, Esqr., Septem-
ber 6, 1736, the aforesaid 50 acres of land was petition-
ed for as lapsed for non-payment of quitrent and
granted to Robert Bratton from John Harmon. Ad-
joining William Lewis. April 2, 1773.
Thomas Poage, 98 acres, being part of Beverley Manor.
April 2, 1773.
Robert Young, 550 acres, at head of Falling Spring Branch,
a branch of Middle River. Adjoining John Poage, Beverley Manor, Robert King. Dec. 8, 1772.
John Patterson, 254 acres, Middle River, part of 390 acres
first granted to John Patterson by patent June 1, 1750.
Adjoining John Wood, George Lewis. Dec. 12, 1772.

## Page 207

Christopher Wagoner, 400 acres, Head Branches of Long Meadows, a branch of the North Branch of Shenandoah. Adjoining Thomas Bryant, Reuben Harrison. July 14, 1772.

George Lewis, 106 acres, Middle River. Adjoining Robert Read, John Patterson, William Oldham, William Hamilton. December 9, 1772.

James Anderson, 137 acres, Head Spring of the Long Glade. Adjoining Samuel Curry. December 5, 1772.

Hugh Donohue, 1227 acres, Naked Creek. Adjoining Robert McCutchen, John King, John Seawright, William Blair. Mentioned James Leeper. June 18, 1773.

## Page 208

John Poage, 650 acres, Middle River. Adjoining Robert Young, James Anderson, James Allison, William Hamilton, John Patterson. Mentioned Robert King, William Sharp, John King. January 7, 1773.

Thomas Connely, 250 acres, branch of Middle River. Adjoining John Campbell, Alexander Walker, John McMahan, Hugh Donahue, Hooks. March, 1773.

John Burnside. Adjoining The Stone Meeting Houseland, Samuel McKee and his own land. January 2, 1773.

Andrew McComb, 40 acres, branch of Naked Creek. December 24, 1772.

## Page 209

David Gibson, 260 acres, Drafts of Naked Creek. Adjoining John Stepheson, John King, Andrew McComb. November 27, 1772.

Edward Moal, 216 acres, Head Branches of Smiths Creek. Adjoining Robert Williams, Henry Armentrout, George Armentrout, Charles Divers. January 11, 1773.

Jacob Bear, 363 acres, Middle River. Adjoining John Givens, Samuel Henderson. January 6, 1773.

John Givens, Jr., 97 acres, Middle River. Adjoining William Lamb, Benjamin Yeardley, and his own land. January 6, 1773.

John Dunkle, 50 acres, South Branch of Potomac. Adjoining Ludwick Waggoner, Mathew Patton, and his own land. October 14, 1772.

Mathias Lehan, 182 acres, Linvills Creek. Jan. 15, 1773.

James Patterson, 36 acres, Middle River. Adjoining John
Patterson, John Young. February 1773.

## Page 210

William McDowel, 69 acres, lying on the limestone ridge
near Smiths Creek. Adjoining his old corner, Sehorns.
January 12, 1773.

William Dunlap, 70 acres, Middle River. Adjoining John
Dixon, James Kerr, Beverley line. Feb. 12, 1773.

James Kerr, 97 acres, Middle River. Between Christians
Creek and Meadow Run, a corner of Beverley Manor.
Adjoining John Dixon. February 12, 1773.

Francis McBride, 29 acres, Brocks Creek. Adjoining his
own land, Samples. February 17, 1773.

William Davis, 130 acres, Brocks Creek. Adjoining John
Phips, Michael Ford. February 18, 1773.

Michael Ford, 88 acres, Brocks Creek. Adjoining John
Phips, Samuel Conner. February 18, 1773.

## Page 211

John Thomas, 98 acres, branch of Brocks Creek. Adjoining
Bordens. February 19, 1773.

Conrod Custard, 40 acres, Brocks Gap. February 19, 1773.

John Runyon, 98 acres, Brocks Gap. February 20, 1773.

Michael Hover, 190 acres, Brocks Gap. February 20, 1773.

Thomas Bagg, 138 acres, Brocks Gap. February 22, 1773.

Nicholas Lamb, 245 acres, Brocks Gap. Adjoining Thomas
Bagg. February 22, 1773.

## Page 212

Adam Bible, 159 acres, Hungary Run, Brocks Gap. Adjoining James Logan. February 23, 1773.

James Lowry, 145 acres, Hungary Run, Brocks Gap. Adjoining Adam Bible. February 23, 1773.

James Logan, 82 acres, Hungary Run, Brocks Gap. Adjoining James Lowry, Adam Bible. February 23, 1773.

Charles Mann, 71 acres, Brocks Gap. Feb. 24, 1773.

John Compton, 93 acres, Core Run, Brocks Gap. Feb. 24,
1773.

Paul Custard, 59 acres, Brocks Gap. Adjoining John Miller.
February 24, 1773.

William Fitzwater, 23 acres, West Gap. Adjoining John
Keplinger, Thomas West. February 25, 1773.

Phillip Keplinger, 33 acres, West Gap. Adjoining Henry Westall. February 25, 1773.

Thomas West, 40 acres, West Gap. Adjoining Charles Mann, John Fitzwater. February 25, 1773.

### Page 213

Michael Keiler (Kaylor) 150 acres, between the Shenandoah River and the Peaked Mountain. Adjoining Nicholas Huffman, John Lingle, Harberg. March 11, 1773.

Jacob Peters, 255 acres, branch of Shenandoah River. Adjoining John Fudtche. March 19, 1773.

John Hetrick, 165 acres, Shenandoah River. Adjoining Jacob Mann. March 5, 1773.

Jacob Herman, 200 acres, Stony Run, Branch of Shenandoah. Adjoining Jacob Gross, Patrick Barnet. March 12, 1773.

Peter Angely, 60 acres, Mary Creek, Branch of James River. April 1, 1773.

Henry Monger, 49 acres, Shenandoah River. Adjoining Henry Sellers. March 5, 1773.

### Page 214

Mathias Scarce, 65 acres, Shenandoah River. Adjoining his own land, Henry Monger. March 11, 1773.

Jacob Beryer, 400 acres, South River. Adjoining Casper Beryer, James Craig. March 27, 1773.

James Telford, 268 acres, Irish Creek, branch of James River, March 31, 1773.

James Patterson, 56 acres, South River. Adjoining his own land, James Craig. March 22, 1773.

### Page 215

James Craig, 672 acres, between South River and Middle River. March 26, 1773.

James Craig, 742 acres, South River. March 25, 1773.

### Page 216

John Davidson, 88 acres, South River. Adjoining his own land, Henry Liner, James Craig. March 26, 1773.

Gibert Collams, 254 acres, Head of Irish Creek, branch of James River. March 31, 1773.

John Davidson, 158 acres, South River. Adjoining Christian Clemance, Robert Steen. March 23, 1773.

Peter Asam, 31 acres, Humes Run, branch of Shenandoah.

78 ABSTRACT OF SURVEYS

March 10. 1773.
James Telford, 72 acres, Marys Creek, branch of James
River. March 30, 1773.
Joseph Sorrel, 150 acres, South River. March 23, 1773.

Page 217

Christopher Nacob, 24 acres, Calfpasture River. April 21,
1773.
Samuel Hamilton, 45 acres, Cowpasture River. April 23,
1773.
Martin Sea, 62 acres, Calfpasture River. Adjoining his own
land, Bratton. April 22, 1773.
John Gay, 46 acres, Cowpasture River. Adjoining James
Gay. April 24, 1773.
John Carolile, 50 acres, Bullpasture River.
George Bratton, 45 acres, Jacksons River. May 7, 1773.
William Willson, 92 acres, Mill Creek, branch of Jackson
River. May 7, 1773.

Page 218

Robert McMillan, 340 acres, branch of Potomac River. Ad-
joining Joseph Gamble. May 1, 1773.
James Bradshaw, 76 acres, Bullpasture River. March 29,
1773.
Robert Carolile, 65 acres, Bullpasture River. April 30, 1773
John Ramsey, 95 acres, Calfpasture River. Adjoining Alex-
ander Cracket, James Cracket. April 23, 1773.
Alexander Dole, 77 acres, Carrs Creek, branch of James
River. November 3, 1772.

Page 219

Thomas Hicklin, 85 acres, Bullpasture River. Adjoining
James Bradshaw. March 29, 1772.
Robert McMullen, 125, acres, Bullpasture River. Adjoining
Robert Duffel. May 3, 1773.
Abraham Hempenstall, 60 acres, Bullpasture River.
John Dickinson, 95 acres, Cowpasture River. Mentioned
Donnelys Ridge. April 26, 1773.
John Douglas, 145 acres, Branch of the Potomac. Adjoin-
ing John Jordan. May 3, 1773.
David Dick, 60 acres, Calfpasture River. Adjoining Bever-
ley. April 21, 1773.

Page 220

Charles Donnely, 75 acres, branch of Cowpasture River. April 26, 1773.

Edward Thompson, 217 acres, Cowpasture River. Adjoining William Thompson. April 27, 1773.

Robert Wiley, 78 acres, branch of Jackson River. May 6, 1773.

David Taylor, 270 acres, branch of Potomac. May 3, 1773.

John Willson, 60 acres, Jackson River. May 6, 1773.

Ralph Laverty, 45 acres, Cowpasture River. April 26, 1773

Page 221

Samuel Willson, 86 acres, Bullpasture River. Adjoining his own land, Tully Davitt. May 3, 1773.

Tully Davitt, 58 acres, Bullpasture River. Adjoining Samuel Willson. May 5, 1773.

John O'Neal, 82 acres, Bullpasture River. Mentioned Caroliles land. May 6, 1773.

George Skillern, 36 acres, Jackson River. May 6, 1773.

Robert Duffell, 49 acres, branch of Bullpasture River.

Page 222

John Cartmell, 140 acres, Cowpasture River. Mentioned John Carmell, Sr., Samuel Cartmell. April 24, 1773.

Martin Stophelmire, 180 acres, Forks of Naked Creek, branch of Shenandoah. Adjoining William Monger. March 8, 1773.

Felix Gilbert, 63 acres, between Cub Run and Peaked Mountain. Adjoining his own land. Feb. 7, 1773.

Samuel Beaty, 110 acres. Adjoining John Fraizer. May 17, 1773.

Page 223

George Keplinger, 133 acres, West Gap, on a branch called George's Run. February 25, 1773.

Martin Westall, 50 acres, West Gap. February 26, 1773.

Jacob Mizel, 54 acres, Bennets Run a branch in West Gap. February 26, 1773.

John Kaplinger, Sen., 52 acres, West Gap. Adjoining Martin Westall. February 23, 1773.

George Lewis, 143 acres, Bennets Run, West Gap. Adjoining Jacob Mizell.

Martin Westall, 87 acres, West Gap. Adjoining John Keplinger.

Page 224

Nicholas Weatherholt, 455 acres, Mud Lick, branch of West Gap. February 27, 1773.

John Ruble, 75 acres, South Fork, West Gap. Feb. 24, 1773

Joseph Desponet, 189 acres, Parting Run, West Gap. February 27, 1773.

Nicholas Weatherholt, 22 acres, Head of West Gap. Adjoining Fairfax line, Michael Moyer. March 1, 1773.

Martin Westall, 25 acres, West Gap. March 1, 1773.

Michael Moyer, 178 acres, Head Spring of Joes Creek in West Gap. Beginning at Weatherholt's corner on Fairfax line. Adjoining Desponet, Burgar. March 1, 1773.

Henry Switzer, 126 acres, Head of West Gap. Adjoining Jacob Mizell.

Page 225

Solom Goodpasture, 70 acres, Fineses Creek, Brocks Gap. March 3, 1773.

John Dunbar, 60 acres, Brocks Creek. Adjoining Samuel Nicholas. March 4, 1773.

Phillip Dalley, 150 acres, North Fork of Shenandoah. Adjoining his own land, Shoemaker, Chrisman. March 5, 1773.

Henry Kirk, 152 acres, Martin Run, branch of North Fork of Shenandoah. Adjoining Dalley, Whitmer. March 5, 1773.

John Peterscern, 76 acres, North Fork of Shenandoah, near Brocks Gap. Adjoining John Whitmer, Michael Hover (Hoover). March 5, 1773.

Adam Reder (Rader), North Fork of Shenandoah. Adjoining his own land. March 6, 1773.

Page 226

David Laird, 68 acres, Head of Collins Lick Branch. Adjoining Robert Scott, Mathew Thompson. March 30, 1773.

John Massey, 227 acres, North River. Adjoining Hugh Donohue.

List for Coledge and County made out this fair. June 21, 1773.

Hugh Donahue and James Hooks, 164 acres, North River. Adjoining John Massey, John Campble. July 8, 1773.

Jacob Lingle, 33 acres, Shenandoah River. Adjoining Boyer and his own land. March 11, 1773.

George Neegley, 142 acres. Adjoining Michael Armicost. April 11, 1774.

Page 227

Samuel Erwin, 167 acres, Middle River. Adjoining James Allen, Barbara Smith, William Oldham, William Hamilton. July 1, 1773.

Nehemiah and Josiah Harrison, 636 acres, Head Draft of Cooks Creek, including two tracts ye one containing 370 acres granted to Jeremiah Harrison by patent the 10th of February, 1748, the other tract contains 135 acres granted to said Harrison by patent the 20th of September, 1768. Adjoining Henry Ewin, Alexander Miller. July 7, 1773.

John Herdman, 119 acres, West Fork of Cooks Creek. Adjoining his own land, Henry Ewin, Harrison, Alexander Miller. July 7, 1773.

Henry Ewin, 128 acres, Head Draft of the West Fork of Cooks Creek. Adjoining his own land, Harrison, John Herdman, William Ewin. July 7, 1773.

Joseph Patterson, 50 acres, Highest Draft of Naked Creek. Adjoining his father's land, John Francis, William Young. July 10, 1773.

Page 228

Henry Stone, 90 acres, Black Thorn, branch of Potomac. Adjoining Christopher Owe. July 6, 1773.

James Hogg, 170 acres, Black Thorn, branch of Potomac. Adjoining Mark Swadley, Bastain Hover. July 5, 1773

Henry Peninger, 98 acres, South Branch Potomac. July, 1773.

Joseph Bailey, 185 acres, Black Thorn, branch of Potomac. Adjoining Mark Swadley, James Hogg. July 4, 1773.

David Bell, 113 acres, Black Thorn, branch of Potomac. July 7, 1773.

Abrham Smith, 170 acres, Crab Apple Bottom. Adjoining Peter Hoal. July 27, 1773.

Jasper Goodenborg, 33 acres, South Branch of Potomac. July 1773.

John Euing, 19 acres, Head Draft of the West Fork of Cooks Creek. Adjoining William Shannon. July 8, 1773.

Charles Smith, 62 acres, South branch of Potomac. July 4, 1773.

82	ABSTRACT OF SURVEYS

## Page 229

Authorized by a warrant dated the 25th November 1773
under the hand and seal of his Excellency The Earl
of Dunmore Governor of Virginia, I have surveyed for
George Washington, Esq., 2813 acres of part (3000
acres granted by the above warrant) of land in Augusta County lying on some Branches of Shirtee Creek
a branch of the Ohio. Charles Morgan and William
Haneson, chain carriers. William Crawford, agent.
Returned to my office ye 25th May, 1774. Thomas Lewis, S.
A. C.

(Note by P. C. Kaylor) : Before Washington received
a patent for the 3000 acres granted him by the Earl of Dunmore and Governor of Virginia by proclaimation of 1763,
England deprived him (Washington) of all his estate be-
yond the Alleghanies.

John McClanahan, assignee of James Walker, 2000 acres,
Monongahela River in Augusta County, being part of
a warrant for 3000 acres which the said James Walker
is intitled to by his Majesties proclaimation of 1763.
March 6, 1774.

## Page 230

John McClanahan, assignee of James Walker, 1000 acres
lying on the Monongahela River in Augusta County,
being part of the above said warrant to take up 3000
acres. March 1, 1774.

## Page 231

John McClanahan, assinee of Captain Charles Scott, 1000
acres in Augusta County, lying on the Monongahela
River. April 1, 1774.

## Page 232

John McClanahan, 2200 acres in three tracts on the Monongahela River. March 10, 1774.

## Page 233

Peter Hog, 3000 acres, Monongahela River in two tracts.
April 25, 1774.

## Page 234

James Kerr, 130 acres, Middle River. Adjoining William
Robertson, Edward Rutlege, Beverley line near Christian Creek. October 14, 1773.

William Hynds, 300 acres, Middle River. Adjoining Thomas Turk, Barrier, Margaret Hinds, October 15, 1773.

Hugh Allen, 400 acres, Middle River.    Adjoining Samuel Hinds, Harless. October 15, 1773.

William Kerr, 70 acres, Middle River.   Adjoining Edward Rutledge, Hugh Allen, Samuel Hind. Oct. 13, 1773.

Cutlip Gabbart, 50 acres, South Branch of Potomac. Adjoining Henry Swadley. October 21, 1773.

George Rexroad, 53 acres, South Branch of Potomac. October 21, 1773.

## Page 235

Henry Stone, 73 acres, South Branch of Potomac. October 21, 1773.

Robert Davis, 48 acres, South Branch of Potomac. October 22, 1773.

Andrew Gongle, 17 acres, Peter Reeds Creek, a branch of South Branch of Potomac. October 25, 1773.

Joseph Briggs, 45 acres, South Branch of Potomac. October 26, 1773.

William Gragg, 200 acres, Seneca Creek. October 27, 1773.

Andrew Johnston, 30 acres, South Branch of Potomac. Adjoining George Teeter. October 28, 1773.

Paul Teeter, 43 acres, South Branch of Potomac. October 28, 1773.

James Cunningham, 85 acres, South Branch of Potomac.

Adam Moser, 50 acres, South Branch of Potomac. Adjoining Shelton. October 30, 1773.

## Page 236

John Wees, 76 acres, South Mill Creek, South Branch of Potomac. November 1, 1773.

John Stutler, 97 acres, South Mill Creek, South Branch of Potomac. November 1, 1773.

Nicholas Mitchcar, 80 acres, South Branch of Potomac. November 1, 1773.

Phillip Croits, 97 acres, South Branch of Potomac. November 2, 1773.

Hugh Murphie and Jacob Conrod, 92 acres, South Branch of Potomac. Adjoining Thomas Parson. Nov. 3, 1773.

Adam Lough, 80 acres, Shavers Run, branch of South Fork of Potomac. November 3, 1773.

Margaret Hind, 194 acres, branch of Middle River.    Ad-

joining Adam Dunlap, William Hind. Nov. 12, 1773.
Adam Dunlap, 185 acres, branch of Middle River. Adjoining James Kennerly. November 12, 1773.

## Page 237

Thomas Moore, 5 acres, Smiths Creek. Adjoining John Phillips and his own land. October 6, 1774.
Cornelius Riddle, 192 acres, Linville Creek. Adjoining David Robenson, John Brunk, Hunter. Sept. 5, 1774.
Alexander Miller, 173 acres, Muddy Creek. Adjoining Gawn Hamilton, John Hinton. April 29, 1774.
John Lilley and John Benson, 300 acres, North Fork of Shenandoah. Adjoining Aaron Hughes, John Stalp, Mathias Lair. June 6, 1774.
George Clerk, 150 acres, Head Branches of Smiths Creek. Adjoining David Laird, Robert Samples, William Hains, George Carpenter. May 24, 1774.

## Page 238

George Carpenter, Sr., 150 acres, Head Branches of Cub Run. Adjoining David Laird and his own land. May 24, 1774.
John Carpenter, 110 acres, branch of Cub Run. Adjoining his father and Henry Bushong. May 27, 1774.
Leonard Miller, 145 acres, North Fork of Shenanoah. Adjoining his own land, Jasper Faught. May 24, 1774.
Gawn Hamilton, 125 acres, between Muddy Creek and Dry River. Adjoining Alexander Miller. April 29, 1774.
Cornelius Riddle, 335 acres, branch of Long Meadow, North Fork of Shenandoah. Adjoining Mathias Lair and his own land. May 5, 1774.
Dawson Wade, 24 acres, Bullpasture River. Dec. 11, 1767.
    Note: The above transferred to William Stuart for non-payment of fees, per Michael Brown, Sheriff.

## Page 239

Alexander Wells, and Nathan Cromwell both of the Country of Baltimore in the Province of Maryland, 2000 acres, lying in the County of Augusta in the forks of Gross Creek, a branch of the Ohio. Henry Wells and James Homes sworn as Chainmen. January 18, 1775.
Sarah Gibbs, 200 acres in the County of Augusta, lying on a small branch of Hard Bargain Creek, a branch of

the Ohio. Adjoining Herman Greathouls in the Cove. January 18, 1775.

## Page 240

John Stepsenson, 25 acres, Naked Creek. Adjoining the East side of the land he lives on which said land with a larger tract was formerly surveyed for William Blair but on a petition to ye Honorable the Council in June 1773 an order passed which instituted said Steph enson to survey out of said Blair's tract 25 acres so as to include his spring and improvements. Dec. 22, 1774. Note: by P. C. K. this land is the farm of Dr. E. A. Herring on Mill Creek.

Henry Miller and Mark Byrd, 1150 acres, Mossey Creek. Adjoining Francis Erwin, Robert Curry, Abel Griffeth. Mentioned Ketrick. September 20, 1774.

Thomas Adams, 545 acres, Calfpasture River. Adjoining Robert Gays, William Campbell, William Lockridge, July 15, 1774.

## Page 241

Lewis Circle (Zircle), Smith Creek. Adjoining Andrew Huland, John Philips. June 3, 1774.

Isaac Gum, 220 acres, branch of Back Creek above Lewis' land. April 29, 1774.

Daniel McNare, 525 acres, Middle River and Jennings Branch. Adjoining George Moffett. February 9, 1775.

Thomas Cockran, 400 acres, between Jennings and Moffett Branch. Adjoining Michael Hogshead, James Campbell, John Hogshead. April 5, 1775.

## Page 242

William Cragg, 64 acres, Seneca Creek. Dec. 10, 1774.

Thomas Campbell, 150 acres, Seneca Creek, branch of South Branch of Potomac. Adjoining William Gragg. Dec. 12, 1774.

Robert Stephenson, 74 acres, South Branch of Potomac. April 25, 1775.

John Stephenson, 396 acres, branch of Naked Creek. Adjoining Robert McCutcheon, John King, and his own land. December 22, 1774.

Michael Armicost, 315 acres, branch of South Branch of Potomac. Adjoining George Neighley, Sickinfoot. April 11, 1774.

Michael Armocust, 174 acres, branch of South Branch of Potomac. Adjoining Abraham Smith, Cunningham. April 13, 1774.

### Page 243

Valentine Server (Sevier), 386 acres, Long Meadows. June 5, 1769.

John Biard, 923 acres, Jennings Branch. Adjoining Thomas Biard, George Moffett, James Campbell, Mathew Eames, John Archers. February 10, 1775.

John Benson, 230 acres, North Fork of Shenandoah River. Adjoining Frederick Kaylor, Fairfax line, George Bowman. June 4, 1774.

Richard Shanklin, 108 acres, Cooks Creek. Adjoining his own land, Windle Butts. February 21, 1774.

### Page 244

Robert and Andrew Nicholl, 270 acres, Moffett's Branch. November 25, 1774.

Jacob Peck, 340 acres, Falling Spring. Adjoining George King, William Anderson, Sampson Mathews, William Lewis. October 17, 1774.

Francis Gardner, 136 acres, Buffallo Branch. Adjoining his own land, John Wood. October 8, 1774.

John Crawford, 398 acres, Buffillo Branch. Adjoining John Wood, Phillips, William Bell, Francis Gardiner, Sagars. October 28, 1774.

John Brunk, 150 acres, Cedar Run. Adjoining his father's land, James Jackson, John Hunter, Conrod Weeble, John Gratton, Christopher Brunk. November 1 1774.

George Moffett, 160 acres, Jennings Branch. Adjoining Daniel McOnails (or McAnails), John Beard. February 9, 1775.

### Page B-244

John Tanner, 218 acres, Kirteses Creek. Adjoining his own land, Leonard Miller. February 21, 1775.

Mathew Edmiston, 91 acres, Jennings Branch. Adjoining James Campbell, Hogshead. February 11, 1776.

Josiah Davison, 35 acres, Linvile Creek. Adjoining Thomas Bryant, Laiers, Josiah Boon. June 8, 1774.

Josiah Davison, 510 acres, South Branch of Potomac. Mentioned James Wood. April 19, 1774.

John McMahan, 330 acres, between Middle and North River. Adjoining Margaret Frames, Walkers. February 23, 1775.

John Poage, 200 acres, South Branch of Potomac. Adjoining Samuel Willson.

John Archer, 50 acres, between his own and Bradshaw's Branches. November 24, 1774.

### Page 245

Alexander Wells, 200 acres, Ohio River, generally called Mingo Bottom, opposite the old Mingo Town on the said River. Mentioned Sarah Gibbs, John McNeely. June 6, 1775.

David Shippherd, 940 acres, branch of the Ohio River. Mentioned Francis Kertley. November 10, 1774.

Nathaniel Blackmore, 300 acres, Shirtee Creek, a branch Of the Ohio, about one half mile below Frowmans Mill. Thomas Cook and Daniel Leet, chainmen. May 10, 1776

### Page 246

William Cromwell, 1700 acres, Shirtee Creek. May 10, 1776

John Campbell, 50 acres, near Pittsburg. Beginning at a stone in the Great Road at the corner of Roderick Frances field, thence to a walnut on the bank of the Alegany River. Mentioned Peter McCockey. May 20, 1775.

John DeCamp, 200 acres, Shirtee Creek, about a half mile above where the Old Mingo Path crossed said Creek. Adjoining James Crig, Banfields. Mentioned Joseph Abrahams. June 11, 1776.

### Page 247

David Shipherd, 1060 acres, upon the works of Weeling about five miles from the mouth where it falls into the Ohio River. November 1774.

Mathew Ritchie and William Bruce, 1307 acres, Shirtee Creek. Adjoining Rankin, William Price, Marcus Stephenson. January 28, 1775.

Mathew Ritchie and William Bruce, 693 acres, on the waters of Kings Creek. January 28, 1775.

### Page 248

George Washington, 587 acres, Ohio River, at a place called the Round Bottom. March 28, 1775.

John Gibson, 500 acres, Ohio River. March 15, 1775.

## Page 249

Richard Yeats, 1000 acres, Shirtee Creek. March 15, 1775.

John Madison, Jr., 3000 acres, branch of Ohio River. Mar. 15, 1775.

John Cannon, 1000 acres, Shirtee Creek. January 10, 1775.

## Page 250

John Nevil and Valentine Crawford, 2000 acres, Shirtee Creek. Adjoining Craigs Bottom. January 20, 1775.

## Page 251

Robert Rutherford, 2500 acres, Racoon Creek. April 7, 1775.

Thomas Rutherford, 500 acres, Short Creek, branch of Ohio. April 9, 1775.

## Page 252

Walter Powers, 185 acres, Irish Creek, a branch of James River. March 1, 1775.

Geroge Taylor, 85 acres, Irish Creek. February 29, 1775.

Robert Edmundson, 170 acres, Irish Creek.

George Berry, 84 acres, Middle River.

Robert Knox, 88 acres, Bullpasture River. March 15, 1775.

## Page 253

Thomas Boyd, 80 acres, Marys Creek, branch of James River. Adjoining Samuel Steel, Robert Campbell. March 3, 1775.

John Trimble, 204 acres, Panther Mountain on the waters of Irish Creek. March 3, 1775.

John Trimble, 73 acres, Mill Creek, branch of Great Calfpasture River. May 18, 1775.

John Lyle, 290 acres, Irish Creek, Adjoining Gilbert Colloms. March 2, 1775.

Hugh Kelso, 60 acres, Walkers Creek, branch of James River. Adjoining James Walker, John Willson. March 7, 1775.

## Page 254

Sampson Christian, 180 acres, Calfpasture River. March March 8, 1775.

Theophilus Blake, 95 acres, Cowpasture River. March 9, 1775.

Andrew Dannelly, 116 acres, Cowpasture River. March 10, 1775.

Robert Shields, 68 acres, Cowpasture River. Mar. 10, 1775.
David Fame. 76 acres, Cowpasture River.
George Adam Bright, 400 acres, Mary Creek, a branch of
the North Branch of James River. Adjoining Thomas
Boyd, Robert Campbell. March 14, 1776.

Page 255

Richard Harrison, 465 acres, Mononghela River. Adjoining
Charles Martin. April 19, 1774.
Charles Martin, 790 acres, Mononghela River. April 19,
1774.
Gasper Everly, 490 acres, Mononghela River. Adjoining
Richard Hanison, Charles Ramseys, Harrison. April
21, 1774.
John Hamilton, 356 acres, Mononghela River. April 25,
1774.

Page 256

John Snider, 250 acres, Mononghela River. Adjoining
Charles Martin, Richard Harrison. April 19, 1774.
David Scott, 658 acres, Mononghela River. April 22, 1774.
Charles Ramsey, 350 acres, Mononghela River. Adjoining
Richard Harrison. April 21, 1774.

Page 257

Jacob Scott, 387 acres, Mononghela River. Adjoining David
Scott. April 25, 1774.
James Scott, 480 acres, Mononghela River. April 23, 1774.
Thomas Day, 280 acres, Mononghela River, Adjoining
Richard Harrison. April 19, 1774.
John Carter, 327 acres, Mononghela River. April 28, 1774.

Page 258

John Evans, 285 acres, Mononghela River. Adjoining
James Johnson. April 20, 1774.
James Johnson, 280 acres, Mononghela River. April 20,
1774.
James Stockwell, 150 acres, Mononghela River. Adjoining
George Hart. April 27, 1774.
Michael Cairns, 615 acres, Mononghela River. May 3, 1774.

Page 259

George Hart, 220 acres, Mononghela River. Adjoining John
Evans. April 27, 1774.
Richard Lamaston, 400 acres, Mononghela River. Adjoin-

ing John Clyne, George Hart, John Evans. April 27, 1774.

John Clyne, 400 acres, Mononghela River. Adjoining John Carter, James Stockwell. April 20, 1774.

Thomas Parsons, 340 acres, Cheat River, opposite to and above the upper end of Horse Shoe Bottom. April 12, 1774.

## Page 260

James Parsons, 714 acres, branch of Cheat River. April 12, 1774.

Thomas Cushman, Jr., 628 acres, Cheat River. Adjoining Ephraim Frazee. May 14, 1774.

Joseph Robenet, 400 acres, branch of Cheat River. Adjoining John Maurice. May 13, 1774.

## Page 261

Jacob Herlin, 800 acres, branch of Cheat River. May 9, 1774.

Martin Judy, 525 acres, branch of Cheat River. May 10, 1774.

Ephriam Frazze, 234 acres, branch of Cheat River. May 10, 1774.

John Maurice, 580 acres, branch of Cheat River. May 13, 1774.

## Page 262

Richard Maurice, 730 acres, branch of Cheat River. May 14 1774.

Thomas Moore, 400 acres, branch of Cheat River. May 12, 1774.

Samuel Warrel, 550 acres, branch of Cheat River. May 14, 1774.

John Hartness, 394 acres, branch of Cheat River. May 15, 1774.

## Page 263

Noah Rude, 387 acres, branch of Cheat River. Adjoining Charles Donelson. May 12, 1774.

Anthony Worldley, 300 acres, branch of Cheat River. Adjoining Richard Maurice. May 14, 1774.

James Dinwiddie, 382 acres, branch of Cheat River. May 11, 1774.

Charles Donleson, 400 acres branch of Cheat River. May 11, 1774.

Arthur Gorden, 365 acres, branch of Cheat River. May 9, 1774.

Page 264

Amos Mills, 395 acres, Dunkard Creek, branch of the Mononghela. November 3, 1774.

Enock Enocks, 400 acres Dunkard Creek, branch of the Mononghela. November 3, 1775.

William Elliott, 400 acres, Tygarts Valley, a Fork of the Mononghela. November 16, 1775.

George Shellener, 310 acres, between the Shenandoah River and the Blue Ridge. Adjoining Fraizers Run. February 4, 1777.

Page 265

James Parker, 31½ acres, Mary Creek. April 19, 1777.

William Mathews, 560 acres, Moffetts Branch. Adjoining his own land, Adam Reaburns. November 24, 1774.

David Mathews, 150 acres, Seneca, branch of South Branch of the Potomac. Adjoining William Gregg. December 12, 1774.

William Armstrong, 238 acres, Jennings Branch. Adjoining Samuel Morras, Robert McKitrick, Robert Armstrong. October 27, 1774.

Mathew Patton, 17 acres, Jackson River. Septemebr 7, 1774

Page 266

Henry Heath, 1320 acres, South Branch of the Potomac. April 18, 1775.

William Heath, 200 acres, South Branch of the Potomac. Adjoining Joseph Bennet, April 17, 1775.

John Hogshead, 257 acres, Bradshaws Creek. Adjoining William McKeney, David Hogshead. April 5, 1775.

David Hogshead, 53 acres, Bradshaws Creek. April 6, 1775.

Bryant Keney, 80 acres, Jennings Branch. Adjoining Michael Hogshead, Robert McKetrick, Hugh Johnson. April 5, 1775.

Barnet Lance, 400 acres. Adjoining James Cunningham, Abraham Smith, Christopher Waggoner. Dec. 20, 1774

Henry Heath, 1320 acres, South Branch of Potomac, April 18, 1775.

William Heath, 200 acres, South Branch of Potomac. Adjoining Joseph Bennet. April 17, 1775.

John Hogshead, 257 acres, Bradshaws Creek. Mentioned

James Hogshead, David Hogshead, Adjoining William McKenney, David Hogshead. April 5, 1775.

David Hogshead, 53 acres, Bradshaws Creek. April 6, 1775

Bryant Keney, 80 acres, Jennings Branch. Adjoining Michael Hogshead, Robert McKitrick, Hugh Johnson. April 5, 1775.

Bryant Lance, 400 acres. Adjoining James Cunningham, Abraham Smith, Christopher Waggoner. April 20, 1776.

### Page 267

John Given, 50 acres, Middle River. Adjoining Samuel Henderson, Patrick Crawford. March 25, 1775.

Abraham Smith and John Skidmore, 390 acres, South Branch of the Potomac. Adjoining Peter Hoal, April 14, 1775.

Abraham Smith and John Skidmore, 193 acres, South Branch of the Potomac. Adjoining Peter Hoal, William Lewis. April 14, 1775.

John Skidmore, 290 acres, Crab Apple Bottom. April 11, 1775.

John Poage and John Skidmore, 400 acres, South Branch of the Potomac. April 15, 1775.

Robert Davis, 312 acres, South Branch of the Potomac. April 18, 1775.

### Page 268

Barnet Lance, 395 acres, Crab Apple Bottom. Adjoining William Cunningham, Jacob Tross. April 12, 1774.

Barnet Lance, 98 acres, Crab Apple Bottom. April 12, 1774

John Brunk, 160 acres, Ceder Run on the West side of Linvils Creek. Adjoining Joseph Lemon, Henry Bear, James Thomas, John Jackson. May 3, 1774.

Michael Warren, 250 acres, Drafts of Linville Creek. Adjoining Elihu Mossey. May 8, 1774.

Henry Collier (Coaler or Kaylor), 186 acres Cortess Run (Kirteses Creek. Adjoining William Lamb and his own land. February 20, 1775.

Samuel Vance, 150 acres, Jacksons River. July 7, 1774.

### Page 269

Andrew Lair, 135 acres, Long Meadow. Adjoining Thomas Bryant, Benson. May 6, 1774.

James Ewin, 122 acres, Middle River. Adjoining John Mc-

Clung. Robert Patterson, Mathew Wilson, Samuel Mc-
Clung. March 2, 1775.
Abraham Smith, 198 acres, Crab Apple Waters. April 11,
1774.
Job Renolds, 200 acres, South Branch. Adjoining Anthony
Johnston. April 27, 1775.
John Cawhey, 213 acres, Walkers Run, branch of Middle
River. Adjoining John Burnside, Thomas Frames,
John Campbell, John McMahan. July 16, 1775.
John Lemon, 225 acres, Brock Creek. Adjoining John
Thomas, Samuel Conner, Michael Fords. May 2, 1774.

Page 270

William Perigan, 300 acres, Drafts of West Cook Creek.
Adjoining Jeremiah Harrison, Jeremiah Ragan, John
Harrison, Henry Ewin. May 11, 1774.
Jacob Dickison, 173 acres, South Branch. Adjoining Josiah
Davison, Charles Smith. April 19, 1774.
Abraham Boyer and Peter Coons (Koontz), 150 acres,
Long Meadows. Adjoinining Thomas Lookey, Thomas
Moore. June 7, 1774.
Christopher Eye, 180 acres, South Branch. Adjoining Hen-
ry Stone. April 11, 1775.
George Buffingbauer, 35 acres, South Branch. April 21,
1775.
George Sithes, 97 acres, South Mill Creek. April 21, 1775.
Henry Pukle, 150 acres, South Branch. Mentioned Jasper
Egart. April 24, 1775.
Peter Smith, 110 acres, South Branch. April 27, 1775
Nicholas Simmon, 50 acres, South Branch. April 27, 1775.
George Simmon, 83 acres, South Branch. April 27, 1775.
Henry Stone, 63 acres, South Branch. April 27, 1775.

Page 271

Andrew Hamilton, 187 acres, Calfpasture River. April 29,
1775.
Thomas Brown, 190 acres, Middle River. Adjoining Bever-
ly, John Phillips. March 1, 1775.
Hugh Johnson, 30 acres, Jennings Branch. Adjoining John
Hogshead, Bryant Kenney. February 12, 1775.
John Vance, 54 acres, Jackson River. April 7, 1774.
Mary Gregory, 188 acres, Jackson River. Mentioned James
Cunningham. April 8, 1774.

James Kerr, 400 acres, Adjoining his own land, Thomas
  Stuart, Samuel Black. November 25, 1774.
William Lewis, 200 acres, Middle River. Adjoining George
  Beverly. October 17, 1774.
Adam Reabrum, 30 acres, Bradshaws Branch of Middle
  River. Adjoining William Mathews. Nov. 24, 1774.

### Page 272
Thomas Rutherford, 1000 acres, branch of Racoon Creek.
  William Hughland, pilot.
Henry Hughland and James Hughland, C. C. April 3, 1775.
Thomas Rutherford, 1000 acres, Ohio River. April 2, 1775.
Randal Slack, 160 acres, Black Thorn. Adjoining Christo-
  pher Eye.
Joseph Bennet, 25 acres, South Branch. April 13, 1774.

### Page 273
John Robinson, 385 acres. April 23, 1751.
John Robinson, 182 acres, a part of 100,000 acres on Green-
  brier River. April 19, 1751.

### Page 274
John Robinson, eight different tracts of land, being part of
  the 100,000 acres. April 24, 1751.

### Page 275
John Robinson, nine different tracts of land, being part of
  100,000 acres. April 30, 1751.

### Page 276
John Robinson, eight different tracts of lang, being part of
  100,000 acres. April 27, 1751.

### Page 277
Andrew Lewis, 500 acres, Greenbrier River. Oct. 21, 1751.
John Robinson, 420 acres, Ewings Creek. April 27, 1752.
John Brown, 550 acres ,branch of Greenbrier River called
  Ewing's Creek. April 9, 1752.
John Brown, 270 acres, Greenbrier River, April 9, 1752.
John Robinson, 285 acres, Greenbrier River. May 3, 1752.
William Gregory, 50 acres, Back Creek. April 8, 1774.
James Ewing, 370 acres, Locust Bottom, Greenbrier River.
  October 22, 1751.

### Page 278
Robert Worthenten, 1873 acres, on the old Mingo Path on

the Waters of Raccoon Creek. May 10, 1774.
Fredrick Hanger, 600 acres, Branch of Greenbrier River.
November 1, 1752.
Felix Gilbert, 250 acres, Branch of Greenbrier River. (Part
of John Robinson Esq. order of council to take up
100,000 acres). Adjoining William Grags. Oct. 25,
1751.
Peter Hanger, 150 acres, Mudy Creek. April 24, 1751.
Samuel Carrel, 250 acres, Anthonys Creek. Adjoining Sam-
uel Hemphill. October 25, 1751.

## Page 279
Alexander Wright, 385 acres, Greenbrier River. April 23,
1751.
William Hopkins, 600 acres, Greenbier River. Oct. 24, 1751
Archebald Hopkins, 260 acres, Greenbrier River. Oct. 26,
1751.
John See, 250 acres, Greenbier River, Oct. 21, 1751.
Edward McMullen, 335 acres, Greenbier River, April 17,
1751.
John Robisen, 270 acres, Greenbrier River. May 2, 1751.

## Page 280
Samuel Howard, 950 acres, Greenbrier River. April 10,
1751
William Hambleton, 323 acres, Greenbrier River. Oct. 16,
1751
William Rennick, 215 acres, Greenbrier River. Oct. 11, 1751
Phillip Rambaugh, 212 acres, Greenbrier River. Nov. 1,
1752
Andrews Lewis, 175 acres, Greenbrier River. Dec. 10, 1754
Patrick Davis, 140 acres, Greenbrier River. April 10, 1751

## Page 281
Mathew Braken, 130 acres, Greenbrier River. May 10, 1769
William Blair, 105 acres, Greenbrier River. April 10, 1769
Andrew Crocket, 363 acres, Greenbrier River. May 8, 1769.
Nathaniel Day, 300 acres, Greenbrier River, April 26, 1769.
Joal Fletcher, 115 acres, Greenbrier River. May 1, 1769.
James Hugart, 260 acres, Greenbrier River. May 5, 1769.
Hugh Galaspy, 230 acres, Greenbrier River. May, 1769.

## Page 282
James Nox, 105 acres, Greenbrier River. May 10, 1769.

Robert Nox, 95 acres, Greenbrier River. May 10, 1769.
Charles Hannison, 205 acres, Greenbrier River. April 25,. 1769.
William Kenny, 200 acres, Greenbrier River. May 8, 1769.
William Lewis, 540 acres, Greenbrier. April 22, 1769.
John Lewis, 66 acres, Greenbrier River. April 20, 1769.
Hugh Johnson, 162 acres, Greenbrier River. May 5, 1769.
Laurence Murphey, 115 acres, Greenbrier River. May 4,. 1769.
James McCoy, 100 acres, Greenbrier River. May 4, 1769.

Page 283
William Man, 485 acres, Greenbrier River. May 9, 1769.
William McCoy, 160 acres, Greenbrier River. May 4, 1769
John McCoy, 70 acres, Greenbrier River. May 4, 1769.
William Man, 110 acres, Greenbrier River. 1769.
Moses Moon, 44 acres, Greenbrier River. April 19, 1769.
Thomas Raferty, 270 acres, Greenbrier River. April 26,. 1769.
John Robison, 390 acres, Greenbrier River. May 2, 1769.
William Renicks, 156 acres, Greenbrier River. April 29,. 1769.

Page 284
William Sharp, 355 acres, Greenbrier River. April 21, 1769
Thomas Williams, 105 acres, Greenbrier River. May 5, 1769.
Joseph Williams, 105 acres, Greenbrier River. May 10, 1769
John Gratton, 915 acres, North River of Shenandoah of
    Brocks Gap, 576 acres part of thereof being originally
    granted by patent to Benjamin Bordin. March 4, 1773.
Jasper Faught, 300 acres, North River of Shenandoah. Ad-
    joining his own land. May 24, 1774.

Page 285
Charles Lewis, 580 acres, Greenbrier River. May 3, 1769.
John Robison, 810 acres, Greenbrier River. May 1, 1751.
Beneyah Rice, 220 acres, Dry Fork of Shenandoah in the
    North Mountain. May 1, 1774.

# BOOK OII

## Page 1

George Boswell, 220 acres. Adjoining Hugh Donoho, Lewis April 5, 1780. William Campbell, Nathaniel Scott, Chain carriers.

Hugh Donoho, 206 acres, between South River and South Mountain. Adjoining Glaves, Hannah, Boswell. April 4, 1780.

Jacob Scott, 150 acres, between Glaves land and South Mountain. April 5, 1780.

George Boswell, 182 acres, Madison Gap. April 7, 1780.

John Freazer, 62 acres. Adjoining Grubbs, William Hooks, Mathew Thompson, Kerrs. April 11, 1780.

William Hook, Jr., 112 acres. Adjoining Robert Shanklin, Robert Hook, Hudlow, James Hook, Perkeys. April 12, 1780.

Andrew Hudlow, 34 acres, Stony Lick Run. Adjoining Robert Scott. April 12, 1780.

## Page 2

John Peters, 360 acres, Wolf Run. Adjoining Jacob Peters. April 20, 1780.

John Heney, 200 acres, Swift Run. Adjoining Hans Maggot, William Smith and crossing Great Road. April 19, 1780.

Henry Hernsberger, 30 acres, Shenandoah River. Adjoining his own land, Kertly, Peterfish. April 19, 1780.

William Nole, 150 acres, Hawksbill. Adjoining Hans Maggot, Boughman. April 21, 1780.

Augusteen Price, 170 acres. Adjoining Peter Miller (Jacob Persinger, Argenbright, Francisco. April 29, 1780.

George Mallow, 186 acres, Adjoining Sniders, Hermans. May 12, 1780.

## Page 3

John Davis, 562 acres, Mossey Creek. Adjoining David McComes, Francis Ewins, McCaumis, Hugh Douglass, Joseph Douglass, McVeyes. May 17, 1780.

John Crawford, 363 acres, Briery Branch. Adjoining James Davis, Wildon, Thomas King, Donelson's Survey, Malcom. May 6, 1780.

## Page 4

John Grattan, 508 acres, North River. Adjoining Hares, Josiah Cunay, Erenomus Deck, John Olivers, Donaho, Lush. April 20, 1780.

Charles Shouls, 312 acres, Dry Fork of Smiths Creek. Adjoining Reuben Harrison, Coffman's Survey. April 14, 1780.

Walter Crow, 216 acres, Head Draft of Linvill Creek. Adjoining his own land. Leonard Herron's survey, Jerry Ragan, Frazurs, Eversole, Crone. April 15, 1780.

Engle Boyer, 516 acres, Smiths Creek. Adjoining John Armstrong, Haga, Reuben Harrison, William Henton's survey, Laurance Bell. March 30, 1780.

## Page 5

Seriah Stratton, 160 acres, South Branch of the Potomac. Adjoining Samuel Scidmore. May 25, 1780.

John McGill, 242 acres, North River. Adjoining James Munay, William Herring, Snodden. May 19, 1780.

James McGill, 220 acres, North River. Adjoining the land he lives on, Francis Ervin, John Davis.

Archibald Hopkins, 262 acres, Muddy Creek. Adjoining Shanklin and the land he lives on. May 21, 1780.

## Page 6

David Ralston, 48 acres, Linville Creek. Adjoining Leonard Herring, Daniel Stover. March 22, 1780.

Robert Mathews, 23 acres, Linvils Creek. Adjoining Vance Coplin, Leonard Herring. March 22, 1780.

Leonard Herring, 88 acres, Drafts of Linvills Creek. Adjoining Walter Crow, John Crow. March 22, 1780.

John Hopkins, 90 acres, South Branch of the Potomac. Adjoining George Kele, Woolf, Shelton. April 14, 1780.

Michael Waring, (Warren) 120 acres, Long Meadows Drafts. Adjoining Bryants. April 14, 1780.

Thomas Spencer, 196 acres, Beaver Creek. Adjoining Henry Miller formerely Hendersons, Olivers, Abraham Smiths formerly Minicks. May 3, 1780.

## Page 7

Joseph Smith, 114 acres, Dry River. Adjoining Andrew Johnson. May 14, 1780.

Joseph Duglass, 75 acres, Head Drafts of Fishers Spring. Adjoining his own land formerly Boyds, John McVeys. May 19, 1780.

Francis Erwin, 230 acres, North River. Adjoining the land he lives on, Samuel Erwin, John Davis.

John Ewin, 27 acres, Linvills Creek. Adjoining Brown, Samples, John Blain. March 24, 1780.

Uriah Gartin, 86 acres, Dry River. Adjoining James Shannon, Benjamin Harison formerly Edwardses. May 13, 1780.

### Page 8

Reuben Harrison, 198 acres, Big Spring a branch of Smith Creek. Adjoining Ray. April 15, 1780.

Ingle Buyer, 56 acres, Branch of Smiths Creek. Adjoining John Harrison, Armentrout, Robert Dickey. March 31 1780.

Felex Shelpman, 32 acres, Cooks Creek. Adjoining Thomas Harrison, Redafords, Daniel Smiths. May 24, 1780.

Hugh Diver, 170 acres, Mossey Creek. Adjoining Henry Miller, Ervins, John Davis, McCaumis, Thomas Reads. May 18, 1780.

Hugh Diver, 210 acres, North River. Adjoining Miller's land formerely Henderson's Silas Hart. May 18, 1780.

### Page 9

James Diver, 585 acres, Briery Branch. Adjoining Henry Miller formerly Henderson's, Isiah Shipman, John Smith. May 5, 1780.

John Smith, 150 acres, Beaver Creek. Adjoining Isiah Shipman, James Diver. May 4, 1780.

Benjamin Kinly, 208 acres, on Antonies spring a branch of Linvills Creek adjoining, Townsend Mathews, Ewins, Mill place. March 23, 1780.

Benjamin Kinly, 178 acres, Muddy Creek. Adjoining Hopkins. May 22, 1780.

### Page 10

Benjamin Kinly, 250 acres, on Antonies Spring a branch of Linvills Creek. Adjoining Townsend Mathews. March 23, 1780.

Ezekiel Harriso, 30 acres, East Branch of Cooks Creek. Adjoining Thomas Harrison, Hemphell. April 25, 1780

Christopher Horn, 280 acres, Dry Fork of Smiths Creek.

Adjoining Townsend Matthews, Reuben Harrison.

John Haneson, 65 acres, West Fork of Cooks Creek. Adjoining Thomas Haneson, Miller, Thomas Harrison. April 25, 1780.

Christopher Horn, 400 acres, Dry Fork of Smiths Creek. Adjoining Woolfs. April 14, 1780.

Michael Sitler, 106 acres, Smiths Creek. Adjoining Daniel Smiths. April 13, 1780.

Page 11

Brewer Reeves, 324 acres, Long Meadows. Adjoining Valentine Sever, Holsinger. April 11, 1780.

Daniel Smith, 210 acres, Dry Fork of Smiths Creek. Adjoining Reuben Harrison, Horn. April 15, 1780.

Daniel Smith, 88 acres, Drafts of Dry Fork. Adjoining Darby Ragan, Felix Shalpman, John Shelpin, Richard Ragan. April 14, 1780.

John Herdman, 230 acres, between the Headwaters of Linvills and Cooks, Creek. Adjoining John Ewins Cabbin place, Jackson, Shannan, Thomas Campble, John Brown. March 24, 1780.

Page 12

Valentine Sever, 200 acres, Long Meadows. Adjoining John Moore, Hanesons. April 10, 1780.

Thomas Reeves, 300 acres, Long Meadows. Adjoining Brewer Reeves, Michael Holsinger. April 11, 1780.

Anthony Reader, 68 acres, branch of Fort Run. Adjoining Phifer, Adam Reader, April 10, 1780.

Jacob Senger, 38 acres, between Cooks Creek and North River. Adjoining Shanklins. May 13, 1780.

Tunis Vanpelt, 8 acres, Dry Branch of Linvills Creek. Adjoining John Crow, Robison. April 26, 1780.

John Haneson, 100 acres, Dry Fork of Smiths Creek. April 29, 1780.

Page 13

Michael Warin, 280 acres, Drafts of Linvils Creek. Adjoining Shouls. April 28, 1780.

John Grattan, 268 acres, Cooks Creek. Adjoining Francis Stuart, Mullin, William Lamb, William McGill. Widow Cravins, Quins, Herrings. May, 1780.

Benjamin Harrison, 260 acres, Drafts of the West Fork of Cooks Creek. Adjoining Alexander Miller, Love. May

12, 1780.
John Craig, 400 acres, Lawyer's Road. November 21, 1780.
Jeremiah Harrison, 84 acres, Drafts of Dry Fork. Adjoining Vanversens, Conrads. April 29, 1780.
Jeremiah Harrison, and John Harrison, 340 acres, Smiths Creek. Adjoining Robert Samples, David Harnets. April 29, 1780.

### Page 14
Samuel Short, 215 acres, Shenandoah River. Adjoining Fulches, John Breedin. March 17, 1781.
Anthony Oylor, 80 acres, Adjoining Huffman, Windle Buts Richard Shanklin, Fishers. April 4, 1781.
Hugh Donoho, 90 acres, North River and Naked Creek. Mentioned Grattan. April 5, 1781.
Nicholus Poss, 70 acres, North River. Adjoining Tootwiler, John Oyler. April 4, 1781.
George Pence, 215 acres, Drafts of Cub Run. Adjoining Adam Pence, Kyger, John Craig, John Perky, George Pence. April 13, 1769.
John Laufer, 190 acres, Smiths Creek. Adjoining William Henton, John Helfrey, John Armentrout, Zebulon Harrison, Needhams. January 3, 1782.

### Page 15
Archebald Hopkins, 177 acres, Muddy Creek. Adjoining Shanklin. April 8, 1782.
Michael Holder, 136 acres, Stony Lick Run. Adjoining John Frazures, Michael Moyers, February 8, 1782.
Thomas Bowin, 100 acres. Adjoining Green, Heaton, 1782.
Martin Argabright, 250 a c r e s. Adjoining Seawright, Shrums. March 9, 1782.
Martin Argabright, 120 acres, Adjoining his own land and Taylors. 1782.
John Helphrey, 100 acres Smiths Creek. Adjoining William Henton, Armentrout. January 3, 1782.

### Page 16
Charles Power, 73 acres, South Branch of Potomac. March 9, 1782.
Jonas Heaton, 22 acres. Adjoining Thomas Huston, Greens, David Beny. January 2, 1782.
Moses Cummins, 100 acres, Smiths Creek. Adjoining John Phillips, Lokers. April 3, 1782.

Godfrey Haga, 400 acres, Forks of Smiths Creek. Adjoining Reuben Harrison, David Harnet. Feb. 21, 1782.

Moses Cummins, 220 acres, Smiths Creek. Adjoining Thomas Moore, John Phillips. April 3, 1782.

Ludwick Circle, 220 acres, West side of Smiths Creek. Adjoining Birds, Moore, crossing a Road, Coxes land. February 7, 1782.

John Smith, Jr., 32 acres, Buffalo Branch of South Branch of the Potomac. Adjoining Venaman, Collicks. March 7, 1782.

Page 17

Leonard Painter, 50 acres, Bushes Creek. Adjoining John Tanner, Nelson. February 21, 1775.

Jacob Lincoln, 200 acres, East side of Linvils Creek. Adjoining Robert Belsheer. Surveyed in consequence of Abraham Lincoln entry of 200 acres dated July 14, 1770, and by him assigned to the above Jacob Lincoln. January 2, 1782.

William Clifton, 70 acres, South Branch of the Potomac. March 8, 1782.

Jacob Conrod, 46 acres, South Branch of the Potomac. Adjoining Fawler. March 8, 1782.

Leonard Miller, 140 acres, Stovers Mill Creek. Adjoining Huston. February 13, 1782.

Henry Deck, 50 acres, East side of Curtes (Kirteses) Creek. Adjoining Leonard Painter, Nelson, February 14, 1782.

Henry Stalp, 35 acres, North River, between his own land and Sears. By an entry of his father William Stalp for 100 acres made July 31, 1770. March 29, 1782.

Page 18

Brewer Reeves, 256 acres, Long Meadows. Adjoining Boston Marches (Sebastian Martz) Lookey, March 28, 1782.

Brewer Reeves, 145 acres, Long Meadows. Adjoining Lore, Cox, Sever, Rife, Holsinger. March 27, 1782.

Brewer Reeves, 114 acres, Long Meadows. Adjoining Lookey, Woodly, Linkhorns survey, John Kring. March 27, 1782.

Alexander McFarlin, 278 acres, East side of Big Spring of Smiths Creek. Adjoining Zebulon Harrison, Noxes, January 5, 1781.

Josiah Davison, 80 acres, branch of Linvils Creek. Adjoining James Calhoon, Greens, David Berry. Mentioned Daniel Harrison, George Baxter. January 7, 1782.

### Page 19

George Baxter, 228 acres, North Mountain. Mentioned Ephriam love, Samuel Iron. January 7, 1782.

Daniel Fraily, 12 acres, Smiths Creek. Adjoining McGlamires, Needams. January 4, 1781.

John Kring, 400 acres, East side of Linvils Creek on the West side of Millers round Hill. Adjoining Jacob Lincoln, Belsheer. Surveyed in consequence of an entry for 400 acres made by Abraham Lincoln April 25, 1771, and assigned to said Kring. Surveyed January 3, 1782.

Josiah Davison, 196 acres. Adjoining Baxter. January 8, 1782.

George Baxter, 118 acres. Adjoining Samuel Irons, William Hopkins. January 12, 1782.

Jacob Harper, 48 acres, South Branch of the Potomac. Adjoining Charles Powers, Jacob Friends. March 9, 1782.

### Page 20

Daniel Love, 120 acres. Adjoining his own land, Cravens, McNiecer, John Craven, Robert Craven, John Miller, Boshangs. March 20, 1782.

George Coil, 100 acres, branch of the South Branch of the Potomac. March 12, 1782.

Ephriam Love, 108 acres, North Mountain. Adjoining Baxter. January 12, 1782.

Benjamin Erwin, 30 acres, Long Glade Branch of North River. Adjoining James McGill, Francis Erwin. May 9, 1782.

Daniel Nelson, 20 acres, Cooks Creek. Adjoining John Cravens. January 16, 1782.

Joseph Lair, 66 acres, Millers Round Hill. Adjoining John Reeves, Thomas Briant. January 3, 1782.

Solomon Mathews, 100 acres. Adjoining Coffman, Michael Warren, in the line of Lovers land. January 26, 1782.

### Page 21

John Helfrey and Daniel Frayley, 66 acres, Smiths Creek. Adjoining Zebulon Harrison, Lanfers, Needam, January 4, 1781.

John Heaton, 80 acres, Linvils Creek. Adjoining Samuel Drake. January 4, 1782.

Jacob Smith, 60 acres, Curtises (Kirteses) Creek. Adjoining Henry Deck, Nelson. Frebruary 15, 1782.

Richard Mathews, 300 acres, East side of Mold Hill. Adjoining Miller, Allford. December 19, 1781.

Solomon Mathews, 130 acres, Linvils Creek. Adjoining Hite, Harrison, Robert Mathews, Paterson, Townsend Mathews. January 5, 1782.

Johnson Nelson, 130 acres, Custeses (Kirteses) Creek. Adjoining Henry Deck, Smith, Huston, Hope, Rodearm. February 15, 1782.

Page 22

Michael Tanner, 140 acres, Mill Creek. Adjoining Whittles, Holder, February 16, 1782.

Archabald Huston, 100 acres, Stovers Mill Creek. Adjoining Leonard Miller, February 13, 1782.

Nathan Huston, 175 acres, Stover Mill Creek. Adjoining Allford, Roadarm. February 12, 1782.

Leonard Tutwiler, 100 acres, North River. Adjoining Pace. February 16, 1782.

Jacob Alberman, 100 acres, North Fork of South Branch of the Potomac. Adjoining William Cunningham, Arthur Johnson. March 5, 1782.

Samuel Miller, 215 acres, North East Side of Mould Hill. Adjoining Richard Mathews. Surveyed in consequence of an entry made by his father Alexander Miller. December 19, 1781.

Page 23

Godfrey Bumgarner, 114 acres, North Fork of the Potomac. March 6, 1782.

Jost Hinkle, 22 acres, North Fork of the South Branch of the Potomac. March 5, 1782.

Seraiah Straton, 110 acres, Reeds Creek South Branch of the Potomac. March 7, 1782.

Conrod Smith, 100 acres North side of the Big Spring of Smiths Creek. Adjoining Zebulon Harrison, Reuben Harrison, Smiths Patent. April 2, 1782. Surveyed in consequence of an entry made by said Smith the 22 of December 1774.

William Rice, 200 acres, Dry River. April 12, 1782.

Zebulon Harrison, 137 acres, South side of Smiths Creek.

Adjoining McGlamiries and near Phillips line. April 5, 1782. Entry made by said Harrison November 17, 1770, for 200 acres.

Page 24

Thomas Campbell, 47 acres, Hunters Spring Branch of Cooks Creek. Adjoining John Herdman, Miller. April 10, 1782.

David Robinson, 112 acres, Linvils Creek near Great Road. March 26, 1782.

Thomas Campbell, 200 acres, West Branch of Cooks Creek. Adjoining Ewens, Herdman.

Richard Campbell, 145 acres, North River of Shenandoah on the Draft of Fort Run. Adjoining John Kenestrick, Hites, Raders, Wedner. November 22, 1780.

Jeremiah Beezly, 48 acres, Shenandoah River. Adjoining Lewis Lingle, Maggot. December 30, 1782.

Stophel Amon, assignee of Boston Anstle, 38 acres, between the Peaked Mountain and Shenandoah River. January 1, 1783.

Page 25

Henry Keslinger, assignee of Christopher Keslinger, 9 acres, Quails Run, branch of Shenandoah River. Adjoining Thornhill. January 3, 1783.

Esther Stephenson, executrix of John Taylor, 230 acres by virtue of an entry made January 10, 1771. (Massanutten Springs). January 14, 1783.

Michael Rork, 80 acres, North side of Shenandoah River. Adjoining Lowdabauh Fuloh, Fulche, Owler. February 11, 1783.

Nicholas Fogal, assignee of Stophel Fogal, 54 acres by virtue of an entry for 100 acres dated March 27, 1763, lying on Dry Run between the Peaked Mountains and Shenandoah River. Adjoining Peterfish. February 13, 1783.

William Hook, Jr., 15 acres, Mill Creek. Adjoining Henry Perkey, Shanklins. 1783.

Daniel Price, 143 acres, between the Peaked Mountain and Shenandoah River. Adjoining Branaman. February 13, 1783.

William Pence, 28 acres, between the Peaked Mountain and Shenandoah River. Adjoining Burk, Daniel Price, Geoorge Huppman. February 17, 1783.

Page 26

John Kisling, 43 acres. Adjoining Allstots, Peterfish, Hammer. February 19, 1783.

Daniel Price 49 acres, North West side of Shenandoah River. February 18, 1783.

John Vice, 41 acres, North West side of Shenandoah River. Adjoining Daniel Price, Jacob Ewly. Feb. 25, 1783.

Henry Price, 23 acres, North West side of Shenandoah River. Adjoining Daniel Price, John Vice, Jacob Ewly. February 25, 1783.

Catharine Hersman, executrix of Olery Hersman, 164 acres, between the South Mountain and her own land. Adjoining Stephen Conrod. February 10, 1783.

Augustine Price, Sr., 22 acres, Shenandoah River. Adjoining Peter Tresler, Harmentrout.

Augustine Price, Sr., 191 acres, between Shenandoah River and South Mountain. The line crossed Fraizer Run. March 5, 1783.

Jacob Cowger, assinee of Ludwick Waggoner, 73 acres, South Fork of the Potomac. Adjoining Boston Howver, March 23, 1783.

Page 27

John Byrne, assignee of William Pickern, 173 acres, Pickerns Run, a branch of the South Fork of the Potomac. March 26, 1783.

Christian Rullman, 53 acres, South Fork of the Potomac. Adjoining Henry Swadly. March 29, 1783.

Valentine Castle, assignee of Henry Brock, 27 acres, South Branch of the Potomac. Adjoining Peter Buzard. March 31, 1783.

Roger Dyer, 129 acres, South Fork of the Potomac. Adjoining Mathew Patton.. April 18, 1783.

Phillip Eakard, 103 acres between the South Fork and South Branch of the Potomac at a place called the Sink holes. Adjoining Henry Stoner. April 4, 1783.

Page 28

Joseph Friend, 69 acres, between South Fork of the Potomac and North Moutnain. Adjoining Jacob Harper. March 31, 1783.

Peter Runkle, assignee of Stephen Conrod, 49 acres, Boon Run. Adjoining Peter Conrod, April 9, 1783.

Anthony Breniman, assignee of Peter Conrod, 240 acres, Humes Run. Adjoining Peter Asom. April 8, 1783.

Edward Franklin, assignee of William Vatters, 159 acres, Shenandoah River. Adjoining John Breeden, April 8, 1783.

John Herdman, assignee of Frederick Stoneberger, 141 acres, between the land he now lives on and the Peaked Mountain. Adjoining Michael Kaylor, Jacob Runkle. April 9, 1783.

Joseph Lowdaback, 168 acres, between Peaked Mountain and Shenandoah River. Adjoining John Fulch, April 8, 1783.

Page 29

John Hopkins, Jr., 40 acres, Muddy Creek.     Adjoining Shanklin. January 30, 1783.

Thomas Harrison, and Thomas Hewist, 400 acres, East side of Harrison's other land. Adjoining Samuel Hemphill. March 18, 1783.

William Smith, 80 acres, Dry River. Adjoining Rigs, Hamilton, John Rice. August 4, 1782.

Phillip Waggy, 220 acres, Howel Branch of Beaver Creek. Adjoining Fulton, Smiths, William Stephenson. Mentioned Adam Stephenson, Mark Riggs. April 2, 1783.

Mathias Rader, 100 acres, East side of Brocks Gap River in a place called the Forrest. Adjoining Nave (Neff). December 5, 1782.

Page 30

Daniel Smith, 375 acres, East Branch of Linvils Creek, including Grubs Spring. Adjoining Jerry Ragan, Walter Crow, Eversole, Warren, Bear. April 15, 1780. N. B. The above in consequence of an entry made July 4, 1770.

Daniel Smith, 300 acres, between Branches of Linvils Creek and Dry Fork of Smiths Creek. Adjoining Norton, Ragan. April 20, 1780.

Ingle Bowyer, 60 acres, Dry Fork of Smiths Creek. Adjoining Bell, Harrison, Sellers. February 20, 1782.

Samuel Seidmore, 180 acres, South Branch of the Potomac on Seidmores Mill Run. March 11, 1782.

Henry Smith, 400 acres, Beaver Creek. Adjoining Andrew Johnson, Josiah Shipman, near a Road. The above in consequence of an entry by Abraham Smith, deceased, and willed to Henry Smith for 400 acres dated February 3, 1769. May 3, 1782.

Solomon Mathews, 115 acres, Head drafts of Long Meadows. Adjoining Michael Warans, Briant. August 12, 1782.

## Page 31

Adam Phifer, 250 acres, North Shenandoah River, in a place called the Forrest. Adjoining Rader, Lare. December 4, 1782.

Adam Orbock, 200 acres, North Shenandoah River, in a place called the Forest. Adjoining Phifer. December 4, 1782.

Mathias Lare, 48 acres, Brocks Gap River. Adjoining Roberson, Stolps. December 5, 1782.

John Bowman, 10 acres, Place called the Forrest, near Fairfax line. Adjoining Benson, Kipps. Dec. 6, 1782.

John Minick, 100 acres, Foot of North Mountain near the Forrest. Adjoining John Whitener. December 7, 1782.

Henry Bower, 35 acres, Brocks Gap River. Adjoining Kitmer, Whitener, Minick, Hatner. The above entry made by said Bower December 24, 1776, for 400 acres. December 7, 1782.

George Replinger, 26 acres, Brocks Gap. Adjoining Bible, Baggs, Lam. December 10, 1782.

## Page 32

Adam Bible, Jr., 113 acres Dry River of Brocks Gap near the Big Lick. Adjoining Bucklick Mountain. December 11, 1782.

Rudolph Corteelias, 70 acres, West Gap at a place called Doeton Lick. Adjoining Henry Davis. Dec. 12, 1782.

David Price, 160 acres, Brocks Gap on Tunises Creek. December 13, 1782.

Conrod, Hartinger, 20 acres, Forrest. Adjoining John Tomas. December 26, 1782.

John Christman Pap, 82 acres, North River below Brocks Gap. Adjoining Hobers, Bears, Nave. Dec. 26, 1782.

Abraham Miller, 60 acres, Forest. Adjoining Andrew Andrews, Douts. The above entry made by Nathias Dout November 24, 1771, for 100 acres and assigned to said Miller. December 27, 1782.

Richard Ragan, 50 acres, on the Irish Sink Draft. Adjoin-

ing Shelpman, Black, John Harrison. The above entry
made by said Ragan April 14, 1770. for 200 acres. January 28, 1783.

Page 33

Henry Heater, 94 acres, Martin Run, on the North side of
Brocks Gap River. Adjoining Shoemaker, Jacob Ketner. The above entry made by Rudolph Brock. December 28, 1782.

Robert and Reuben Harrison, 70 acres, between branches
of Linvil and Cooks Creek. Adjoining William Petijohn, Ragan. February 5, 1783.

Robert and Reuben Harrison, 186 acres, East side of the
East Fork of Cooks Creek. Adjoining Dicktom, George
Seawright, David Shrum, Cravens. The above entry
made by Daniel Smith and assigned to said Harrisons.
February 13, 1783.

Andrew Gougel, 166 acres, South Branch of the Potomac
on Scidmore Mill Run. March 1, 1783.

Peter Terrel, 70 acres, North Fork of South Branch of the
Potomac at a place called Buffalo Bottom. March 3,
1783.

Joseph Summerfield, 83 acres, North Fork of South Branch
of the Potomac at a place called Moose Lick. March 3,
1783.

Page 34

Robert Minnis, North Fork of South Branch of the Potomac. March 4, 1783.

Joseph Smith, 22 acres, Dry River. Adjoining Duglass,
Eastin. March 4, 1783.

Godfrey Bumgarner, 100 acres, North Fork of South
Branch of the Potomac on top of the Mountain opposite of Robert Minnis. March 4, 1783.

Francis Evick, 118 acres, South Branch of the Potomac.
March 6, 1783.

Seriah Stratton, 82 acres, South Branch of the Potomac.
March 6, 1783.

Henry Smith, 328 acres, Head of Beaver Creek. Adjoining
Fulton, Duns. The entry made by Abraham Smith for
400 acres, June 11, 1771, and bequeathed in his last
will to Henry Smith. April 1, 1783.

Page 35

Uriah Garton, 50 acres, Dry River. Adjoining Herring,

Shannon, Murries. May 12, 1783.

Robert Elliot, 66 acres, Cub Run. Adjoining Taylor, McKinley. May 5, 1783.

Michael Rader, assignee of Andrew Hudlow, 84 acres. Adjoining Lewis Circle, Andrew Bird. May 15, 1783.

Evin Phillips, 123 acres, between Smiths Creek and the Mountain. Adjoining John Phillips, Lewis Circle. May 15, 1783.

Robert Williams, 240 acres, Draft of Smiths Creek. Adjoining Valentine Smith, David Laird, Eligah McCalister. November 26, 1782.

Archibald Hopkins, 150 acres, Muddy Creek. Adjoining Ewin Mill place. May 20, 1783.

## Page 36

James Diver, 400 acres. Adjoining King, Crawford, John Wilson, Silas Hart, Hugh Diver. March 22, 1783.

James Diver, assignee of John Crow, 122 acres. Adjoining Hugh Diver, Henry Miller, William Bowyer, King. May 22, 1783.

Reuben Harrison, 88 acres, Branches of Smith Creek, June 10, 1783.

James Bruster, 360 acres, Cub Run. Adjoining John Stephenson, John Huston, Gilberts. Mentioned John Scott.

## Page 37

John Huston, assignee of William Campble, 97 acres, Cub Run. Adjoining Wiats survey, Elliots. Mentioned Felix Gilbert and James Bruster. February 8, 1783.

Michael Hanagan, assignee of Thomas Lewis, 180 acres, Forrest. Adjoining Adam Phifer, Phillip Harpints. September 13, 1783.

Gasper Dayger, 340 acres, at a place called the Hazle Hollow. Adjoining John Moore, McDowels, Ridle. September 15, 1783.

David Miller, 76 acres, Forrest. Adjoining Adam Raders. September 15, 1783.

Charles Calihan, 190 acres, Claylick and War Branch of Muddy Creek. Adjoining Hintons, Hamilton, Henries, Joseph Hinton. March 3, 1783.

## Page 38

Nicholas Harvey, 93 acres, on South Mountain on Gilgo

Run. Adjoining Davis, Edward William. Oct. 30, 1783.

Henry Armentrout, assignee of Conyers White, 312 acres, on the South Mountain. Adjoining Peters Oct. 31, 1783

Henry Stolp, 19 acres. Adjoining David Roberson. September 16, 1783.

Phillip Harpint, 92 acres, Forrest. Adjoining Cooks. Sept. 13, 1783.

Abraham Miller, 28 acres, F o r r e s t. Adjoining Hites, Browns, Nestrick, Campfield.

William Allford, 49 acres, Dry River. Adjoining Stephenson, Lackey, Anthony Curtner. Mark Riggs. September 11, 1783.

## Page 39

Isiah and William Curry, 332 acres, between North Mountain and North River. Adjoining John Stunkard, Pearcey, John Malcom, John Willson, Silas Hart. November 21, 1783.

William Pence, 90 acres, between Peaked Mountain and Shenandoah River. Adjoining Daniel Price, Peter Breniman, also Daniel Finks. December 5, 1783.

Jacob Whitmore, 5 acres. Adjoining Henry Keplinger, Henry Black. November 17, 1783.

## Page 40

William Michael, 117 acres. Adjoining George Mann, Augustine Price, Long. November 3, 1783.

Nicholas Boss, 58 acres, North River. Adjoining Hance Cloverfield. November 18, 1783.

Daniel Price, 25 acres, between Peaked Mountain and Shenandoah River. Adjoining Peter Breniman. Dec. 6, 1783

John Tanner, 158 acres. Adjoining Henry Harman, Michael Tanner, Keller, Tuitweller. November 23, 1783.

John Malcom, 167 acres, between North River and North Mountain. Adjoining Curry, John Willson, Daniel Marrow. November 18, 1783.

Jacob Sanger, 155 acres, North River. Adjoining Shanklin, McGill, September 25, 1783.

## Page 41

Robert Cravens, assignee of Samuel Hemphill, 141 acres, between Thomas Harrison and Argenbright. Adjoining Thomas Harrison, Argenbright. December 19, 1783.

Christian Bullman, 47 acres, South Fork of South Branch

of the Potomac. December 16, 1783.

Henry Swadley, 24 acres, South Fork of South Branch of the Potomac. December 16, 1783.

Henry Proops, 92 acres, South Fork of South Branch of the Potomac. December 17, 1783.

Bostle Hoover, 46 acres, South Fork of South Branch of the Potomac. December 15, 1783.

Mark Swadley, 15 acres, South Fork of South Branch of the Potomac. December 15, 1783.

## Page 42

Charles Rush, 343 acres, South Side of Peaked Mountain. Adjoining George Shaver, Guisse, Phillip Haws. April 7, 1784.

Jacob Woodley, 216 acres, Long Meadows. Adjoining Thomas Lackey, Butcher, Joseph Gore. March 13, 1784.

Jacob Woodley, 11 acres, North side of Peaked Mountain. Adjoining his own land, Peter Harman, Harrison. March 15, 1784.

Phillip Armentrout, 70 acres, North side of Peaked Mountain. Adjoining George Armentrout, Grubs. March 12, 1784.

George Armentrout, 77 acres. Adjoinnig George Fridley.

John Rush and Peter Nicholas, 93 acres, south side Peaked Mountain. Adjoining Charles Rush, Guisse. April 7, 1784.

## Page 43

David Laird, 200 acres, Adjoining Gasper Faught. April 18, 1785.

David Laird, 147 acres, some branches of North River. Adjoining Phillip Keplinger, James Beard, Edward Beard, Bell. April 18, 1785.

George Carpenter, 125 acres, between his own land and Peaked Mountain. April 17, 1784.

John Ware, 73 acres, Cub Run. Adjoining Peter Miller, David Laird, David Smith. April 28, 1785.

Mathis Kirsh, 80 acres, between his own land and Gasper Hain. May 25, 1785.

Gasper Hain, 77 acres. Adjoining Mathias Kirsh, Adam Seller. May 25, 1785.

## Page 44

Phillip Hite, 230 acres, Crooked Run, a branch of Shenandoah River. Adjoining John Fulk. April 8, 1783.

James Laird, 56 acres, between the land he lives on and the Peaked Mountain. Adjoining Taylor. April 27, 1785.

Isaac Hinkle, son of Jacob, 188 acres, Allegany Mountain on the head waters of Senica. Beginning at a beech on the South side of the Road leading to Tyger Valley. May 9, 1785.

Jacob Root, 23 acres, South fork of South Branch of the Potomac. May 6, 1785.

Robert Retherford, 50 acres. Adjoining George Keesel, Robert Elliot. April 29, 1785.

Jacob Root, 24 acres, North Fork of South Branch of Potomac. May 4, 1785.

Lasley Mathews, 32 acres, North Fork of South Branch of Potomac.

### Page 45

Joseph Retherford, 252 acres, on the North of John Taylor. Adjoining Thomas Harrison. April 30, 1785.

John Nelson, 225 acres, three tracts, North Fork of South Branch of Potomac. May 4, 1785.

George David Toebly, 253 acres, Quails Run. Adjoining Balser Tickout. May 25, 1785.

John Morris, 182 acres, North Fork of South Branch of Potomac. May 7, 1785.

### Page 46

Ester Stephenson, executrix of John Taylor deceased, 184 acres, between two tracts of land of her own. May 24, 1785.

Jacob Keeper, 100 acres, South Fork of South Branch of Potomac. Adjoining David Props. May 12, 1785.

George Teeter, 194 acres, two tracts, North Fork of South Branch of Potomac. May 9, 1785.

Andrew Johnston, 54 acres, North Fork of South Branch of Potomac. May 10, 1785.

Frederick Armentrout, 125 acres. Adjoining John Craig, Augustine Price, William Michael, George Mann, May 10, 1785.

### Page 47

Zechariah Rexroad, 100 acres, South Fork of South Branch. May 12, 1785.

John Grabill, 78 acres, Cub Run. Adjoining George Carpenter, Frederick Armentrout. April 28, 1785.

John Sholl, 63 acres, North Mountain, branches of North Fork of South Branch. May 10, 1785.

Thomas Bland, 48 acres, North Mountain. May 6, 1785.

John Davis, 144 acres, between his own land and Francis Erwin. June 6, 1785.

Andrew Shanklin, 55 acres, between Jeremiah Ragan and William Patijohn. Adjoining Harrison. May 14, 1785.

### Page 48

Jacob Bargar, 99 acres, South Fork of the South Branch. May 13, 1785.

Joseph Rutherford, Jr., 150 acres, branch of Cub Run. Adjoining Harmentrouts. August 3, 1785.

Mathew Patten, 90 acres, two tracts, South Fork of South Branch. September 7, 1785.

George Keesel, 250 acres, North of his own land. Adjoining Joseph Davis, Joachim Van Ferson (The Dutch Lord) July 30, 1785.

### Page 49

Benjamin Early, 515 acres, two tracts, lying between the Blue Ridge and South Fork of Shenandoah River. Adjoining Jacob Scott, Anthony Lewis, Frederick Stull. May 24, 1783.

Godfrey Swing, 146 acres, on some branch of Cub Run. Adjoining George Carpenter, John Grabill. December 8, 1785.

Lewis Bowyer, 90 acres, branches of Cub Run. Adjoining John Ware. July 29, 1785.

Jacob Spot, 18 acres, Cub Run. Adjoining George Carpenter, George Keesel, January 6, 1786.

### Page 50

Michael Feesle, 293 acres, lying in Rockingham County on the South end of Supping Lick Mountain on a branch of Tunis Creek. February 18, 1785.

John Bright, 10 acres, branch of Smiths Creek. Adjoining Daniel Grubb, John Harrison. March 25, 1785.

Jacob Ketmer, 83 acres, North Mountain. January 7, 1785.

Jacob Ketmer, 117 acres, lying in the County of Rockingham near the North Mountain, joining a late survey of said Ketmer, Trumbo, and Henry Eaters. Jan. 6, 1785.

Lewis Circle, 150 acres, between Smiths Creek and Peaked Mountain. 1785.

ABSTRACT OF SURVEYS                    115

## Page 51

Archabald Hopkins, Jr., 126 acres, North Mountain. Adjoining Rees Thomas. April 5, 1785.

Joseph Biver, 79 acres, between Kirteses and Cooks Creek. Adjoining Nelson, Cravens, William Lamb. March 30, 1785.

Peter Conrod, 260 acres, both sides of Boons Run. Adjoining Peter Runkle, Frederick Michael, Christopher Ammon. April 11, 1785.

Ann Scothern, 107 acres. Adjoining Samples, Claiks, George Harmon, John Harrison. May 30, 1785.

Stephen Conrod, 41 acres, Boons Run. Adjoining John Seller, Deck, Foy, Conrod Young. April 13, 1785.

## Page 52

Jacob Hetner, 140 acres, North Mountain. Adjoining Henry Bower, Henry Eater. January 6, 1785.

Henry Selzer, 125 acres. Adjoining Ekerly, White, Polser, Harrison, Andrew Bird, McDowel, Sehorn. April 25, 1785.

Joseph Rombo, 94 acres. Adjoining Andrew Bird, Harrison, Lewis Circle, Michael Raiders. June 15, 1785.

John Hatter, 35 acres, on Grindstone Hill, near Bagg and Faulk. January 29, 1785.

Josiah Davison, 160 acres. Adjoining George Baxter. April 5, 1785.

## Page 53

Joseph Davis, 24 acres, lying on the east side of the Great Carolina Road. Adjoining George Keesel, Carpenter. March 14, 1785.

Robert Retherford, 14 acres, Cub Run. Adjoining Elliot, Keesel, Laurence. April 15, 1785.

John Ruddall, 33 acres, North Branch of the Shenandoah River near Brocks Gap. Adjoining John Gratton. April 22, 1785.

"All the surveys before this Recorded is in College Settlement extracted and made February 1786 and the account with the full amount viz. L 55. 16. 4 transmitted to the Rev. Mr. Bucehanon of Richmond who has been empowered to receive such accounts and so forth by the B. . . of ye College of Wm. and Mary."

116		ABSTRACT OF SURVEYS

## Page 54

Gabriel Jones, 360 acres. Adjoining Shanklin, John Craig. February 10, 1786.

Felix Gilbert, 23 acres, lying on some drafts of Cub Run. Adjoining his own land, James Bruster, John Huston. April 18, 1786.

Felix Gilbert, 65 acres, lying between his own land and the Peaked Mountain. Adjoining Joseph Retherford. April 11, 1786.

Adam Helpinger, 170 acres, South Fork of the South Branch. January 16, 1786.

## Page 55

Joseph Skidmore, 96 acres, South Branch. Jan. 16, 1786.

Jacob Conrod, 44 acres, on Drafts of South Branch. January 17, 1786.

Joseph Skidmore, 41 acres, on South Branch. Jan. 18, 1786.

Thomas Collick, 170 acres, North Fork of South Branch. January 20, 1786.

George Richael, 70 acres, South Branch. Adjoining Peter Venimon. January 23, 1786.

John Skidmore, 23 acres, South Branch. January 26, 1786.

## Page 56

Henry Perrine, 100 acres, South Branch of Potomac. January 24, 1786.

John Pharis, 100 acres, Skidmores Mill Run. Jan. 25, 1786.

Nicholas Michael, 40 acres, between North Fork and South Branch. January 25, 1786.

Peter Springton, 100 acres, between North Fork and South Branch. January 26, 1786.

James Skidmore, 70 acres, Skidmores Mill Run. January 26, 1786.

Elliot Retherford, 74 acres, Between head Drafts of Smiths and Cooks Creek. Adjoining the late Daniel Smith, John Harrison, John Benson.

## Page 57

George Lough, 62 acres, Switser Gap Run Branch of South Branch. February 16, 1786.

Adam Lough, 138 acres, Switser Gap Run Branch of South Branch. Adjoining Adam Harpole. February 16, 1786.

Charles Hetvick, 60 acres, Drafts of South Branch. February 16, 1786.

Seriah Stratton, 150 acres, Drafts of South Branch. February 17, 1786.

Thomas Willmott, 130 acres, between North Fork and South Branch. Adjoining Joseph Skidmore. February 3, 1786.

## Page 58

Gabriel Coil, Jr., 55 acres, branches of South Branch. Adjoining George Coil. February 13, 1786.

Leonard Bush, 50 acres, Blind Lick Branch of the South Branch. February 17, 1786.

Michael Bush, 53 acres in two tracts, Branches of Reed Creek. February 17, 1786.

Peter Venimon, 100 acres, between North Fork and South Branch. February 18, 1786.

Conrod Lowrey, 150 acres, Cub Run. Adjoining Felix Gilbert, Charles Rush. April 12, 1786.

## Page 59

George Pence, 90 acres, Peaked Mountain. Adjoining George Carpenter, John Ware, John Carpenter, David Smith. May 2, 1786.

Jacob Bushang, 33 acres, Drafts of Cooks Creek. Adjoining Alexander Miller. March 15, 1786.

David Laird, 75 acres, Drafts of Cub Run. Adjoining Adam Faught. May 1, 1786.

Robert Cravens, 100 acres, some Drafts of Cooks Creek. Adjoining Nelson, John Harrison. March 20, 1786.

Dennis Lanchan and Daniel Guin, 100 acres, between the heads of Curtices (Kirteses) Run and Cooks Creek. Adjoining Nelson, Robert Cravens, John Harrison. March 20, 1786.

## Page 60

James Diver, 83 acres, North side of Timber Ridge. Adjoining Joseph Retherford, Robert Retherford, a naked Hill, Thomas Harrison. March 18, 1786.

James Diver, 66 acres, both sides of Timber Ridge. Adjoining Esther Sthephenson, Joseph Retherford, Robert Cravens. March 18, 1786.

David Taylor, 19 acres, Head branches of Smiths Creek and Cub Run. Adjoining James Laird. April 10, 1786.

Michael Shiry, 37 acres, some drafts of Curtices (Kirteses) Run. Adjoining Coler (Kaylor). March 21, 1786.

118 ABSTRACT OF SURVEYS

Adam Argenbright and John Guin, assignees of Samuel Hemphill, 45 acres, lying on some drafts of Cooks Creek. Adjoining Adam Argabright, Dundore, John Guin. March 21, 1786.

Robert and Reuben Harrison, 55 acres, Head Drafts of Linvils Creek. Adjoining Thomas Harrison, John Robinson. John Ewin, Michael Mullin, John Harrison. March 23, 1786.

Page 61

Adam Argabright, 92 acres, Timber Ridge. Adjoining Robert Cravens, James Diver, Martin Argabright. March 22, 1786.

Godfrey Swing, 50 acres, Drafts of Cub Run. Adjoining George Keesell, Joacham Fanferson, Sheets, Robert Elliot, Robert Retherford. April 10, 1786.

Jacob Moyer, 20 acres, Drafts of Shenandoah River. Adjoining Jacob Bare, April 17, 1786.

John Bright, 60 acres, Peaked Mountain. Adjoining George Harmentrout, Kisers. April 10, 1786.

Henry Cowen, 100 acres, Drafts of Smiths Creek. Adjoining Thomas Lockey, George Conrod, James Lockey. April 9, 1786.

Henry Cowen, 87 acres, branch of Smiths Creek. Adjoining James Lockey, Jacob Moses. April 9, 1786.

Page 62

Valentine Kiser, 11 acres, Drafts of Mill Creek. Adjoining William Hooks, Stovers land. June 10, 1786.

Joseph Bier (Byerly), 55 acres, North East side of Certices (Kirteses) Creek. Adjoining corner to said Biers patent, Lanahan, John Hup, Michael Shirey, Reuben Harrison. April 1, 1786.

Frederick Black, 72 acres, on East side of Cooks Creek. Adjoining Huffman, Anthony Oyler and his own land, William Lamb, crossing and recrossing the Great Road. April 1, 1786.

Seriah Stratton, 110 acres, South Branch. Adjoining Joseph Skidmore. June 27, 1786.

Michael Deck, 36 acres, Boon Run. Adjoining Kerkley, Hammer, Nicholas Null. June 13, 1786.

Page 63

Martin Kunce, 85 acres, Smiths Creek. Adjoining his own

land, Woodley. April 8, 1786.

George Carpenter, 11 acres, Drafts of Cub Run. Adjoining George Keesel, Robert Retherford, Harmentrout. June 20, 1786.

Sinclair Kirkley, 30 acres, Shenandoah River. Adjoining his own land, John Munger, Sellers, Nicholas Null. June 14, 1786.

John Kaster, 58 acres, at a place called the Forrest. Adjoining his own land, John Bowman, Harpine, Eurbauh. March 16, 1786.

Thomas Shanklin, 18 acres. Adjoining his own land, Widow Fulton. February 8, 1786.

### Page 64

Michael Warren, 40 acres, Linvils Creek. Adjoining Jacob Harpole and his own land. April 5, 1786.

Isaac Miller, 234 acres, N. E. side of Mole Hill. Adjoining Richard Mathews, Samuel Miller, Andrew Johnson. April 10, 1786.

Conrod Smith, 10 acres, within one mile of the Big Spring of Smiths Creek. Adjoining Reuben Harrison and his own land. April 23, 1786.

William Pickern, 89 acres, Smiths Creek. Adjoining his own land, Thomas Lockey, crossing the Great Road. April 28, 1786.

Conrod Smith, 156 acres, Long Meadows. Adjoining Reuben Harrison, Thomas Briant, and his own land. April 27, 1786.

### Page 65

John Pitman, 306 acres, Fort Run, a branch of the North Shenandoah. Adjoining Braham M i l l e r, Shutter, Campfield, Martin Roop, John Nestrick. March 17, 1786.

John Apler and John Hicks, 146 acres, branch of Cooks Creek. Adjoining Harrison, Shanklin, Pettijohns, Samuel Miller, John Miller. 1786.

Michael Kip, 58 acres, Forest. Adjoining John Bowman, Fifers, Anthony Rader. March 14, 1786.

Solomon Mathews, assignee of David Rolston, 224 acres, Joes Creek. Adjoining his own land, Frances Green. 1786.

Isaac Miller, 117 acres. Adjoining his old patent. February 10, 1786.

## Page 66

Archebald Hopkins, 102 acres. Adjoining his old patent, Widow Fulton, Thomas Shanklin. February 9, 1786.

Robert Cravens, 74 acres, Cooks Creek. Adjoining Hester Cravens, Quin, Dickton, crossing a Great Road, Daniel Love. March 30, 1786.

John Petner, 109 acres, at foot of North Mountain. Adjoining Meanicks, Adam Wine, John Nestricks, Abraham Miller. March 16, 1786.

Richard Kester, 100 acres, Brocks Gap, Church Mountain. Adjoining Paul Kester, Michael Baker. March 20, 1786.

Peter Vanpelt, 100 acres, Linvils Creek. Adjoining Tunis Vanpelt, John Ewin, Mesicks. April 6, 1786.

## Page 67

Joseph Brigs, 125 acres, branches of Reeds Creek. Crossing Harpers Path. January, 1786.

Joseph Friend, 75 acres, South Branch. Adjoining John Dicer, Jacob Conrod. January, 1786.

George Null, 150 acres, Naked Creek. Adjoining his own land. September 25, 1786.

Henry Null, 100 acres, Naked Creek. Adjoining his own land Jacob Moyer. September 25, 1786.

Adam Faught, 70 acres, Yeagers Branch of Smiths Creek. Adjoining his own land, David Laird, Robert William. April 17, 1786.

## Page 68

Samuel Hemphill, 653 acres, (He having obtained an order of court according to law previous to the making said survey which includes 324 acres of patent land being the greater part of four patents tracts, the first of 123 acres granted sd Robert Cravens 10th February 1748) lying in Rockingham County on a branch of Cooks Creek. Adjoining John Quin, Jeremiah Cravens, John Miller, Ezekel Harrison, crossing Great Road, Thomas Harrison, Martin Argenbright. March 30, 1786.

John Miller, 19 acres, Dry River. Adjoining Gawin Hamilton and his own land. February 7, 1786.

William Nall, 44 acres, Head drafs of Cooks Creek. Adjoining Jacob Bumgarner, Joseph Rtherford. March 17, 1786.

## Page 69
Robert Retherford, 14 acres, branches of Cooks Creek. Adjoining Stover, Harrison, Archer Rutherford. October 10, 1786.
Archebald Hopkins,Sen., 100 acres, Muddy Creek. February 24, 1786.
Thomas Shanklin, 90 acres, between two Branches of Muddy Creek. Adjoining his own land, Archebald Hopkins. February 22, 1786.
Peter Polser, 13 acres, Linvils Creek. Adjoining John Wright, Eversole, Curry. August 29, 1786.
Soloman Mathews, 24 acres, between Linvils and Smiths Creek. August 11, 1786.
Abraham Bird, 89 acres, between Smiths Creek and Masinuting Mountain. April 12, 1787.

## Page 70
Thomas Lewis, 90 acres, N. W. side of Shenandoah River. Adjoining his own land, the late Anthony Lewis, Shanklins, Gabriel Jones. February 12, 1786.
Joseph Hannah, 30 acres. Adjoining his own land, Boswill, Donoho, Turk, Early MaKall. May 11, 1787.
Christian Kyger, 48 acres. Adjoining John Craig, Gabriel Jones. April 9, 1787.
Henry Harmon, 390 acres, Draft of Shenandoah River. Adjoining Peter Rolers, Hans Cloverfield, John Tanner, Windle Buts, Hobbys. May 16, 1786.
James Diver, 36 acres, East Branches of Cooks Creek. Adjoining Thomas Harrisons, Robert Retherford, Bumgarner. March 17, 1786.

## Page 71
Lewis Peopler, 100 acres, Cooks Creek. Adjoining Cravens, Love, Bushang, crossing Great Road, Samuel Miller. March 9, 1787.
Francis Green, 98 acres, Joes Creek. Adjoining three tracts of his own land, Calhoons, Josiah Davison, Ezekiel Green. February 24, 1787.
Lewis Peopler, 20 acres, Cooks Creek. Adjoining Benjamin Smiths, Samuel Hemphill. March 8, 1787.
John Fulk, 48 acres, Brooks Gap. Adjoining Trumbos. June 9, 1787.
Philimon Roack, (O'Roak) 290 acres, between Smiths

Creek and Long Meadows. Adjoining Beaver, Brewer Reeves, John Harrison, Circles. April 13, 1787.

## Page 72

George Springer, 210 acres, between Smiths Creek and Long Meadows. Adjoining Beever, Circle, Thomas Moore, Boston Marche. April 13, 1787.

Nathaniel Shephard Armstrong, 105 acres, between Smiths Creek and Peaked Mountain. Adjoining Wise. May 18, 1787.

William Vance, 66 acres, between Smiths Creek and Long Meadows. Adjoining Reuben Harrison, Charles Shultz March 17, 1787.

Lewis Circle, 30 acres, Smiths Creek. Adjoining Abraham Bird, Phillip Comer. April 11, 1787.

Daniel Fraley, 14 acres, between Smiths Creek and Peaked Mountain. Adjoining Stevens, Griders, Conrod. 1787.

James Diver, 5 acres, within one mile of the Court house. Adjoining Rutherford, Harrison. March 8, 1787.

Benjamin Talman, 5 acres, both sides of Smiths Creek. Adjoining his own land, Daniel Fraley, William Talman. May 10, 1787.

## Page 73

Valentine Sherly, 180 acres, between Shenandoah River and the South Mountain, between Price's and Lewis' land. May 15, 1787.

Peter Wigal, 70 acres, Faught Run. Adjoining Faughts. April 11, 1787.

Charles Hetrick, 48 acres, South Branch. August 7, 1786.

Adam Seller, 290 acres, between Shenandoah River and South Mountain, crossing the Great Road. April 10, 1787.

Valentine Sherley, 420 acres, 220 acres part of the 420 entry made before the Revolution and assigned to him by Felix Gilbert, lying on Fraizers Run at the foot of South Mountain. November 10, 1786.

## Page 74

Jacob Wire, 135 acres, lying near his own land. March 1, 1787.

Joseph Conrod, 100 acres, Drafts of Smiths Creek. Adjoining Ann Scotherns, Harrison. March 19, 1787.

William Clifton, 42 acres, head drafts of Long Meadows.

Adjoining Hamilton. August 6, 1786.
Gawin Hamilton, 64 acres, branch of Muddy Creek. August
3, 1786.
Gawin Hamilton, 400 acres, Buffalo Run Branch of the
South Branch. June 1786.

Page 75
Nathaniel Sheperd, 308 acres, between Smiths Creek and
Long Meadows. Adjoining Conrod Smith. John Reeves
Woodley, Knox, Harrison. May 17, 1787.
Paul Kister, 50 acres, Brocks Gap. Adjoining Marshel.
June 20, 1787.
Reuben Harrison, 30 acres, between Smiths Creek and Dry
Fork. Adjoining Tolmans, Conrods. July 23, 1787.
Michael Baker, 7 acres, Brocks Gap, including the head of
Mill Run. Adjoining Richard Kester, Paul Kester.
June 18, 1787.
Michael Baker, 183 acres, Brocks Gap. Adjoining Richard
Kester. June19, 1787.

Page 76
Conrod Humble, 148 acres, Brocks Gap, Church Mountain.
Adjoining Paul Kester. June 20, 1787.
Reuben Harrison, 150 acres, between Dry Fork and Long
Meadow. Adjoining Conrod Smith. June 30, 1787.
Robert Dickey, 178 acres, between Smiths Creek and Peak-
ed Mountain. Adjoining Friddlies, Lockey, Murry, Morris,
Armentrout. September 3, 1787.
Samuel Gad and David Gilmor, 65 acres, Muddy Creek, be-
low the mouth of Gorden Run, Adjoining Shanklin, James
Gilmore. October 10, 1787.
Henry Henry, 97 acres, between Muddy Creek and War
Branch. Adjoining Hamilton, Henton, Archabald Hop-
kins. February 7, 1786.

Page 77
John Robison, 100 acres, Linvils Creek. Adjoining Elihu
Messick, Samples. March 3, 1783.
Peter Conrod and John Hammer, 64 acres, Dry Run. Ad-
joining Peter Conrod Fish. August 15, 1786.
Seriah Stratton, 50 acres, South Branch. August 18, 1787.
John Makall, 280 acres, between the land of Makall and
South Mountain. Adjoining Thomas Lewis, Hugh Don-
oho, and his own land. April 24, 1787.

124 ABSTRACT OF SURVEYS

## Page 78

Robert Davis, 92 acres in two tracts, between South Fork
and South Branch. April 19, 1788.

Leonard Miller, 60 acres, Bushy Run of Seneca. April 30,
1788.

Jacob Root, 70 acres, North Fork of the South Branch.
April 7, 1788.

Jacob Vandevender, 22 acres, South Run a branch of the
South Branch. April 7, 1788.

John Miller, 50 acres, Props Run, a branch of the South
Branch. April 30, 1788.

## Page 79

James Dyer, 100 acres, Whitsels Run, a branch of the
North Shenandoah. April 18, 1788.

Joseph Bennet, 45 acres, North Fork of the South Branch.
April 9, 1788.

Archibald Hopkins, 56 acres, Muddy Creek. April 30, 1788

Thomas Hall, 75 acres, South Fork of the South Branch.
Adjoining James Dyer, Stephen Miller. April 10, 1788

Wililam Peterson, 80 acres, Roreing Spring Run, a branch
of the North Fork of the South Branch. Adjoining
Cunningham, Minnis. April 30, 1788.

## Page 80

William Darkerty, 300 acres, Brocks Gap. July 26, 1788.

Elizabeth Shanklin, 20 acres, between Muddy Creek and
North Mountain. Adjoining the late John Shanklin.
May 23, 1788.

Abraham Alger, 158 acres, North Mountain. Sept. 29, 1788

William Lamb, 32 acres, Adjoining Beggs, Trumbos, and
his own land. June 5, 1788.

Frederick Black, 20 acres, East side of Cooks Creek. Adjoining his own land, Whanger, Mullins. Oct. 11, 1788.

Martin Grider, 59 acres, Smiths Creek. Adjoining Conrod,
Cowen. March 10, 1789.

## Page 81

Thomas Lewis, 1000 acres, between the land where he lives
and the South Mountain. Adjoining Makall. March 10
1789.

Martin Grider, 146 acres, Smiths Creek. Adjoining Helfrey
George Hermentrout, Rickaback Lockey. March 10,
1789.

John Harris, 50 acres. Adjoining Norton Gum, Mathews, Leaches. March 19, 1788.

John Keplinger, 290 acres, South River in Brocks Gap. July 25, 1788.

Michael Lamb, 100 acres. Adjoining Sittirs, Shoemakers. June 4, 1788.

Page 82

Nicholas Shaver, 30 acres, beginning at two white oaks his and Millers corner, Crombakers. July 6, 1788.

Lewis Stulce, 115 acres, Dry (Tri) River in Brocks Gap. Adjoining Peter Stulce. November 9, 1789.

Christopher Howard, 50 acres. Adjoining Isaac Depo, Shulers, Cratzers, Jacob Harpole, Smith. May 6, 1789.

Jacob Hufft, 84 acres, Fort Run, a branch of the North Shenandoah. Adjoining John Petner, Adam Rader, David Miller. February 9, 1789.

Peter Stulce, 14 acres, Brocks Gap. April 8, 1789.

Frederick Fridley, 28 acres, Smiths Creek. Adjoining Zebulon Harrison, Reuben Harrison, Conrods. May 28, 1789.

Page 83

George Shoemaker, 100 acres, Brocks Gap. April 8, 1789.

Thomas Hopkins, 68 acres, North Mountain. Adjoining George Baxter, John Hopkins. May 8, 1789.

Henny Hartman, 39 acres, Stonny Run in Brocks Gap. Adjoining Simon Shouemaker. April 10, 1789.

Christopher Dupo, 38 acres. Adjoining Michael Sellers, Solomon Mathews, Reuben Harrison. May 6, 1789.

Henry Eater and Henry Shoemaker, 33 acres, North Branch of Shenandoah. April 22, 1789.

Adam Shank, 13 acres. Adjoining Chrisman, Eversole, Mathews, Branaman. April 15, 1789.

Michael Stulce, 54 acres, Brocks Gap. April 9, 1789.

Simon Shoemaker, 39 acres, Stony Run in Brocks Gap. Adjoining Jacob Kertner. April 10, 1789.

John Hermentrout, 36 acres, Smiths Creek. Adjoining Robert Dickey, Munay. March 6, 1789.

Lewis Fulner, 20 a c r e s. Adjoining Chrismans, Dupo, Henry Nave (Neff), Mathew Rader. Feb. 10, 1789.

Page 84

John and Thomas Hopkins, 93 acres, Dry (Tri) River in Brocks Gap. May 8, 1789.

Henry Pup, 20 acrers. Adjoining Bear, Mathias Rader. February 10, 1789.

Mathias Lair, 45 acres, North Branch of Shenandoah. Adjoining Cumbakers, Robison, crossing Great Road, Widow Lair. February 18, 1789.

Mathias Lair, 23 acres, Linvils Creek. Adjoining Widow Lair, Robison. February 18, 1789.

Jacob Zetty, 100 acres, South River in Brocks Gap. Adjoining George Shoemaker, the Great Road, Abraham Miller, Ruddle. April 8, 1789.

John Herdman, 62 acres. Adjoining John Ewin, Henry Ewin, and his own land. March 28, 1789.

Jacob Perkey, 91 acres, on waters of Daniel James branch. Adjoining Henry Kepheart. March 16, 1789.

William Rachford, 50 acres. Adjoining Widow Miller, Isaac Miller. March 28, 1789.

Conrod Peterfish, 11 acres. Adjoining his own land. August 6, 1789.

Mathais Lair, 150 acres, Linvils Creek. Adjoining Jacob Bear, Jacob Rifes, Andrew Bowers. March 20, 1788.

## Page 85

Godfrey Schwing, 270 acres, Drafts of Mill Creek and Cub Run. Adjoining Taylor, Retherford, Vanvarson, (The Dutch Lord), Robert Eliot. March 19, 1787.

George Easterley, 129 acres, Forest. Adjoining Hestons Groves, Folums, Kips, Bowman, Shenandoah County line. March 10, 1788.

Jacob Bare, 70 acres, Linvils Creek. Adjoining Widow Lares, Branamans,

Jacob Trumbo, 50 acres, North Branch of Shenandoah. Adjoining J a c o b Kitners, Christopher Keplingers. April 17, 1788.

"College account made out for all the surveys recorded since my last settlement in June, 1788. And the College proportion of the fees made up and enclosed to Rev. Buchanon. Viz 12-17:8 in interest warrens, also the sum of 12 sh & 3d over and above have credit for this in my next settlement."

John and Henry Pence, 300 acres, lying between the lines of Gabriel Jones, Perkies, Shanklin and Craig. Dec. 9, 1789.

Page 86

Alexander McFarland, 39 acres, between Long Meadows and Smiths Creek, on both sides of a Great Road (Irish Path). Adjoining Thomas Lokey, Reeves, Gores May 29, 1789.

Daniel Dickeson, 263 acres, on some branches of Cooks Creek. Adjoining Harrison, December 31, 1789.

John Meanick, 33 acres, North Branch of the Shenandoah. Adjoining Ketner and his own land. April 15, 1788.

Robert Dickey, 9 acres, branch of Smiths Creek. June 28, 1787.

William Pickering, 23 acres, Smiths Creek. Adjoining his own land, Lokey's McFarland. March 12, 1789.

Page 87

Joseph Davis, 152 acres. Adjoining his own land, The Dutch Lord, Jeremiah Harrison, Joseph Conrod. June 27, 1787.

Henry Nave (Neff), 72 acres. Adjoining Jacob Hufft, Henry Cup, Mathias Rader, Pitner. February 10, 1789.

Jacob Bair, 144 acres, Dry Run. Adjoining his own land. December 10, 1789.

Thomas Camble, 98 acres. Adjoining Cratzer, Solomon Mathews, near Iron Mine, Michael Warren, Shulers. May 6, 1789.

Page 88

Henry Mace, 300 acres, Madisons Gap. Adjoining Makall. November 16, 1789.

Thomas Ogan, 98 acres. Adjoining Eliot Retherford, Benson, Dutch Lord, Hisers, Harrison. April 26, 1788.

Thomas Fulton, 44 acres, Red Bank Run, North Mountain. August 10, 1789.

Page 89

John Woodlie, 96 acres, both sides of Smiths Creek. Adjoining John Phillips, Hilards, Jacob Woodlies, crossing Daniel James branch. November 26, 1790.

Thomas Gorden, 32 acres, Muddy Creek. Adjoining Shanklin, Gilmores. December 15, 1790.

William Smith, Executor of Abraham Smith, 150 acres, on both sides of Briery Branch. Adjoining Craffords, William Devers, Red Banks. December 22, 1790.

William Smith, Executor of Abraham Smith, 44 acres, Island of Dry River. Adjoining Benega Rice. Dec. 1, 1790.

Francis Meadows, 100 acres, at a place known as the Mudhole. Adjoining his own land, crossing the East branch of the Hawksbill to Roacks corner. December 25, 1790

Thomas Moore, 227 acres, between Smiths Creek and Long Meadows. Adjoining Sircle (Zircle) Springer, Marches (Martz), Hoofft, Bird, in consequence of an entry made by Moor, November 30, 1765. January 20, 1791.

John Magat, 238 acres. Adjoining Jacob Maggots, Henry Magots, in consequence of an entry made by David Magot, April 17, 1772. December 20, 1790.

Henry Deck, 20 acres, Curteses (Kirteses) Creek. Adjoining Leonard Painter, Joseph Bier (Byerly), Jacob Deck, in consequence of an entry made by said Deck, July 8, 1777. April 23, 1791.

Joel Smith, heir of Edwin Smith deceased, 400 acres, on the south side of the South River of Shenandoah, in consequence of an entry made for 400 acres by George Conrod, June 12, 1772, and by him assigned to Edwin Smith, December 25, 1779. April 11, 1791.

Martin Countz, 46 acres, Daniel James Branch of Smiths Creek. Adjoining his own land, Murrys, Dickey. December 25, 1789.

John Deneston, 44 acres, Dry River. Adjoining Benega Rice, John Rice. December 1, 1790.

Henry Armentrout, 50 acres, between Smiths Creek and Peaked Mountain. Adjoining John Armentrout, Helfrey, Martin Grider, Steven. December 23, 1789.

George Hoogler and John Vice, 19 acres, South side of North River, between said Hoogler, (Coogler) and Vice. Adjoining McGill. January 8, 1791.

Phillip Countz, 10 acres, Adjoining L o c k e y, Marches (Martz). January 21, 1791.

Benjamin Ewin, 190 acres, part of a tract containing 350 acres granted by patent bearing date September 20, 1748, to John Erven and by him conveyed to said Benjamin Ewin. Lying and being on the Long Glade, a branch of North River, a branch of the Shenandoah. Adjoining Andrew Erven, Wise, McGill, Francis Erven, Samuel Erven, Andrew Erven. May 25, 1791.

## Page 93

Samuel Brown, 17 acres, between Smiths Creek and Long Meadows. Adjoining Jacob Woodley, Goar, Bruer Reeves. February 16, 1791.

Lewis Keller, 125 acres. Adjoining Leonard Miller, Jacob Smith. April 28, 1791.

## Page 94

Lewis Keller, 22 acres, Adjoining Clines (John and Conrod), Leonard Miller. April 28, 1791.

Adam Bott, 13 acres, Curteses (Kirteses) Creek. Adjoining Peter Roler, Windle Botts, Conrod Hulvey. March 18, 1791.

William Herring, 183 acres. Adjoining George Christman, land on the East side of the South River in Brocks Gap November 1, 1790.

Edward Weldon, 40 acres, Briery Branch. November 13, 1790.

## Page 95

Aaron Soloman, 149 acres, between the Long Meadows and Linvils Creek. Adjoining Ezekiel Harrison, Jacob Riffe, Jacob Bowman, John Kring. June 10, 1791.

William Herring, 28 acres. Adjoining Pups, George Rader, Adam Rader, Hooft. February 3, 1791.

Aaron Solomon, 27 acres. Adjoining George Rader, Mathias Will, Henry Pups, Knave (Neff) Hooft. June 2, 1791.

## Page 96

Henry Miller, 411 acres, between Dry River and Beaver Creek. Adjoining Kingery, Devier, Shipman, Benega Rice, Joseph Duglas. May 4, 1791.

Mary Pugh, 150 acres, Bryary Branch. Adjoining Rader. December 20, 1787.

George Harmentrout, 85 acres, branch of Smiths Creek. Adjoining Cepharts, Murry, Counses. Nov. 26, 1790.

## Page 97

William Hinton, 80 acres, between Smiths Creek and the Dry Fork. Adjoining Ray, Bell, Wiat (formerly Needham), Reuben Harrison, and his old tract. June 29, 1787.

Jonathan Shipman, 98 acres. Adjoining Conrods, John Harrison. April 29, 1789.

Frederick Haneker, 70 acres, Main River in Brocks Gap. February 7, 1791.

## Page 98

Paul Quhan, 41 acres, North Shenandoah in Brocks Gap. Adjoining John Compton. December 5, 1789.

Nicholas Fussinger, 81 acres, Tunis Creek in Brocks Gap. December 8, 1789.

Benjamin Smith, 325 acres, Dry River. Adjoining John Rice, James Quins, Joseph Smith. February 10, 1791.

## Page 99

Anthony Rader, 60 acres, Adjoining Adam Rader, Carns. February 1, 1791.

Stephen Harnsberger, 90 acres. Cooks Creek. Adjoining Rader, Sanger, Shanklin, Snodowns. June 7, 1791.

Daniel Gain, 35 acres. Adjoining McDonnel, Edward Shanklin. December 14, 1791.

## Page 100

Isaac Depoy, 50 acres, Dry Fork. Adjoining Turpens, Harrison, and his own land. February 2, 1790.

William Fitzwater, 66 acres, Brooks Gop. Dec. 5, 1789.

John Blaine, 5 acres, Head waters of Linvils Creek. Adjoining Jackson. December 27 1789.

## Page 101

John Blaine, 9 acres, Headwaters of Smiths Creek. Adjoining John Ewin, Jackson, and his own land. December 27, 1789.

James Scott, 47 acres, North Branch of Shenandoah in Brocks Gap, above Christley Keplingers. Dec. 3, 1789.

Nichalas Clark, 66 acres, North Branch of the Shenandoah. Adjoining Fulk. December 7, 1789.

## Page 102

Valentine Woolf, 119 acres, between Dry Fork and Smiths Creek. Adjoining Thomas Harrison, John Harrison, Peter Wheland, Solomon Mathews. Dec. 26, 1789.

John Thomas, 146 acres, South Fork Mountain. Dec. 2, 1789.

Peter Shoemaker, 95 acres, Brocks Gap. December 3, 1789.

## Page 103

Jacob Lingle, 150 acres, South Fork Mountain. Dec. 2, 1790

Michael Sellers, 6½ acres, between Dry Fork and Smiths Creek. Adjoining his own land, Nathaniel Harrison. May 17, 1791.

## Page 104

John Snap, 275 acres. Adjoining his own land, Archebald Huston, Nathaniel Huston, John Allford, Keller, Miller. August 22, 1791.

John Benson, 299 acres, head of the East Draft of Cooks Creek. Adjoining Huses, Archebald Retherford near the Bear Wallow, Jonathan Shipman. Sept. 30, 1791.

## Page 105

John Benson, 190 acres, between the East Draft of Cooks Creek and Dry Fork. Adjoining William and James Smith, Richerford, Benson's New Survey. Sept. 30, 1791.

Jacob Richey, 33 acres, Brocks Gap. November 2, 1790.

Peter Richey, 50 acres, Brocks Gap. Adjoining his patent land, Bagges. November 2, 1790.

## Page 106

Josiah Davison, 114 acrers, between the waters of Linvils Creek and the North Mountain. Adjoining his 365 acre survey, Archebald Hopkins. November 6, 1790.

Josiah Davison, 33 acres, on the waters of Linvils Creek. Adjoining his own land, Calhoon, Green. Nov. 6, 1790.

# INDEX

Claiks O 51
Clark, Nichalas O 101
Clark, John 73
Clayman, Christian 145
Claypole 11
Clencey, James 65, 116
Clerk, George 237
Clifton, Wil'iam 122, O 17, 74
Clines, O 94
Cloverfield, Hance O 40, 70
Cloyd, David 51
Clyne, John 259
Cockran, John 39, 202
Cockran, Thomas 241
Coffman, Survey O 4, 20
Cohnan 87
Cohorn 175
Coil, Gabriel 49, O 58
Coil, George 11, O 20, 58
Coler (See Kaylor)
Collams, Gi'bert 216
College and Country 226, O 53, 85
Collier, Alexander 50, 147
Collier, Henry 268
Collier, Moses 47
Collick, Thomas O 55
Col'ins, Luke 42
Collins, Moses 106
Collins, William 189
Collock, O 16
Colls, Tim 176
Colly, William 77
Colman, 195
Colvin, Joseph 83
Comer, Phillip, O 72
Compton, John 17, 212, O 98
Conley, John 73
Connely, Athen 87
Connely, Authur 195
Conner, Samuel 88, 210, 269
Cook, Cornelius 184, O 38
Cook, Thomas 245
Cook, Valentine 166
Coons (See Koontz)
Cooper, Anthony 56
Cooper, the Dutchman 137
Conrod, George 168, O 61, 91
Conrod, Jacob 202, 236, O 17, 55, 67
Conrod, Joseph, O 13, 72, 74, 80, 87, 97
Conrod, Peter 162, O 28, 51, 77
Conrod, Phillip 169
Conrod, Stephen 3, 168, O 26, 28, 51, 75
Conrod, Zubrick 48
Coplin, Vance, O 6
Corner, Francis 183
Cornerly, Thomas 175, 208
Corteelias, Rudolph, O 32
Coulter, Michael 181

Counts (See Koontz)
Couts, John 179
Couts, Joshua 115
Cowan, William 84, 140
Cowen, Henry, O 61, 80
Cowger, Jacob, O 26
Coxes, O 16, 18
Crab oJseph 82, 80
Cracket, Alexander 218
Cracket, James 218
Craig, Alexander 17
Craig, James 44, 146, 164, 214, 215, 216
Craig, John 30, 145; O 13, 14, 46, 54, 70, 85
Craig, Robert 145
Craig, Samuel 164
Craig, William 67
Craig's Bottom 250
Cratzer, O 82, 87
Cravens, Hester, O 66
Cravens, John 162, 199; O 20 33
Cravens, Joseph 42, 199; O 20, 33
Cravens, Robert 37, 38, 199; O 20, 41, 59, 61, 66
Cravens, Wi'liam 122, 162
Cravens, Widow, O 13
Crawford, Andrew 53
Crawford, George 89, 145, 177, 195
Crawford, Gilbert 13
Crawford, John 71, 156, 244; O 3, 36
Crawford, Josiah 53
Crawford, Patrick 8, 195, 267
Crawford, Valentine 250
Crawford, William 57, 67, 71, 106, 201
Creelys Branch 34
Cresinburg, John 62
Cresswell, Henry 89
Crider, aMrtin, O 72, 92
Crig, James 246
Crocket, Andrew 281
Crocket, Alexander 70, 148
Crocket, Hugh 75
Crocket, Samuel 83
Croits, Phillip 236
Crombaker, O 82, 84
Crone, O 4
Cromwell, Nathan 239
Cromwell, William 246
Crow, John, O 12, 36
Crow, Walter 151, 195; O 4, 6, 30
Crow, William 57, 135
Crun, John 44
Crump, Edmond 108
Cub Run (See Jacob Persinger) 2
Culloms, Gilbert 253

Cummins, John 181
Cunay, Josiah 19, O 4
Cunay, Samuel 164
Cuney, James 195
Cunningham, Agnes 24, 153
Cunningham, Jacob 62
Cunningham, James 122, 154, 193, 235, 266, 271; O 79
Cunningham, Moses 62; O 16
Cunningham, William 184, 190, 191, 200, 268; O 22
Cup, Henry O87
Curry, Isaiah O 39
Curry, Robert 195, 240
Curry, Samuel 207
Curry, William, O 39 40, 69
Curtner, Anthony, O 38
Cushman, Thomas, Jr., 260
Custard, Conrod 211
Custard, Paul 86
Custal, William 94
Cutwright, Peter 52

Dally, Phillip 225
Daniel, Reuben 117
Danny, Patrick 14
Daubin, James 56
Davidson, James 117
Davidson, John 90, 141, 216
Davis, Henry, O 32
Davis, James, O 3
Davis, John 30, 32, 48, 114, 120, 144, 166, 180, 200, 202; O 3, 5, 7, 8, 47
Davis, Joseph 13, 113; O 48, 53, 87
Davis, Robert 163, 235, 267; O 78
Davis, Samuel 36, 121, 133
Davis, William 65, 66, 210
Davison, Josiah 28, 144, 244, 270 O 18, 19, 52, 71, 106
Davitt, Tully 221
Dawson, Henry 150
Day, Nathaniel 281
Day, Thomas 257
Dayger, Gasper, O 37
Dealiss, John 25
Dealy, John 15, 25
Dean, John 52
DeCamp, John 246
Deck, Erenomus, O 4
Deck, Henry, O 17, 21, 91
Deck, Jacob, O 91
Deck, Michael, O 51, 62
Dehart, Simon 76
Delaney, Francis 138
Deneston, John, O 91
Deniston, John 102, 167
Dennis, Joseph 67
Denny, Patrick 36
Depo, Christopher, O 83

Depo, Isaac, O 82, 100
Desponet, 224
Deverick, Thomas 59, 190
Dicer, John, O 67
Dick, David 219
Dick, David 219
Dick, James 45
Dickenson, oJseph 116
Dickey, James 128
Dickeson, Daniel, O 86
Dickey, Robert 142, 152; O 8, 76, 83, 86, 91
Dickinson, Jacob 151, 270
Dickinson, John 37, 39, 54, 63, 69, 89, 201, 219
Dictom, (Joseph?) O 33, 66
Dinwiddie, James 263
Dinwiddie, John 148
Dinwiddie, Robert 148, 149, 187
Diver, Charles 209
Diver, Hugh 117, 197; O 8, 36, 96
Diver, James 118, 156, 196; O 9, 36, 60, 61, 70, 72
Dixon, John 210
Dockerty, George 67, 104
Dockerty, Michael 36, 104
Dockerty, William, O 80
Dole, Alexander 218
Donaho, Hugh 116, 120, 125, 195, 199, 207, 208, 226; O 1, 4, 14, 70, 77
Donald, John 163
Donally, Charles 220
Donally, John 84
Donelly, Andrew 187, 254
Donelly, John 139, 140
Donelson, Charles 263
Donelson Survey, O 3
Dooly, Abraham 71
Dooly, Thomas 71, 165, 179
Douglass, Hugh 197, 201; O 3
Douglass, John 219
Douglas, Joseph 197; O 3, 7, 96
Douglass, Thomas 184
Dout, Mathias, O 32
Downs, Henry 23
Drake, Samuel, O 21
Ducharts, Mary 130
Duff, William 6
Duffell, Robert 124, 219, 221
Doglas, Jonathan 11, 119; O 34
Dun, O 34
Dunbar, John 225
Dundore, O 60
Dunkle, John 18
Dunlap, Adam 236
Dunlap, Alexander 68
Dunlap, John 148
Dunlap, William 210
Dutch Lord, O 48, 85, 87, 88
Dyce, George 157

Dyche, 18
Dyer, George 121
Dyer, James 193; O 79
Dyer, Roger, O 27
Dyerly, James 191
Dyerly, Peter 76, 80, 134, 139

Eager, John 33, 72, 99, 138
Eakard, Phillip, O 27
Eames, Mathew 243
Eariff, Gutlip 129
Eaters, Henry, O 50, 52, 83
Early, Benjamin 3; O 49, 70
East, Josiah 160
Easterly, George, O 85
Eastin, O 34
Edgar, Robert 182
Edmenson, James 13
Edmiston, Mathew 185, 244
Edmundson, Robert 252
Edwards 17
Eiler, Anthony 180; O 14, 25, 62
Eiler, John, O 14
Eiler, William 41
Ekerly, O 52
Elk Run (See Francis Kertly) 3
Ellit, George 153
Elliot, John 89
Elliot, Robert 24, 95, 101, 165; O 35, 37, 44, 53, 61, 85
Elliot, William 264
Elsworth, Jacob 194
Elsworth, Moses 8, 192
Emabaugh, Rudolph 39
Emocks, Mathew 74, 77, 140
English, William 28
Enocks, Enock 264
Erven, John, O 92
Erven, Samuel, O 92
Erwin, Andrew 19; O 92
Erwin, Benjamin, O 20
Erwin, Edward 127, 128
Erwin, Francis, O 7, 20
Erwin, Jane 183
Erwin, Samuel 183, 227; O 7
Estill, Benjamin 66, 99
Estill, Bond, 113
Estill, John 64
Estill, Wallace 13, 64
Euine, Andrew 186
Evans, Alexander 136
Evans, John 258, 259
Evens, Nathaniel 75, 107, 110
Evens, Thomas 76, 98
Evenson, Peter 74
Everly, aGsper 255
Eversole, O 4, 30, 69, 83
Evert, Windle 4, 43
Evins, Amos 98
Evins Daniel 33, 74
Evock, Francis 157; O 34

Evock, George 157
Eweback, Andrew 154
Ewen, Benjamin, O 92
Ewin, Francis 240; O 3, 5, 7,
Ewin, Henry 117, 227, 270; O 84
Ewin, James 269, 277
Ewin, Jarred 87
Ewin, John 38, 151, 180, 228; O 7, 11, 60, 66, 84, 101
Ewin, William 92, 227
Ewly Jacob O 26
Eye, Christopher 117, 196, 270, 272

Fairfax Line 39, 102, 129, 154, 192, 194, 224, 243; O 31
Fame David 254
Faney, Jasper 138
Faney, William 138
Fanferson (See Van Farson)
Farry, Jasper 74
Farry, William 74
Faught, Adam O 59, 67
Faught, Jasper 238, 284; O 43, 73
Feature, Samuel 93
Feesle, Michael O 50
Feeters, George 122
Fifer (See Phifer)
Finchers 122
Finley, George 195
Finley, John 57
Finley, Robert 143, 171
Finley, William 143
Fisher, Peter 169; O 14
Fisher Spring O 7
Fitz, James 60
Fitzwater, John 212
Fitzwater, William 212; O 100
Flesher, Henry 121
Flesher, Peter 198
Fletcher. Joal 281
Floyd, Charles 184
Fogal, Nicholas O 25
Fogal, Stophel O 25
Folum O 85
Forl, Michael 210, 269
Forguson, Henry 33, 74
Forguson, Thomas 139
Foshes, Thomas 138
Foster, William 68
Fouch 3
Fowler, James 156; O 17
Fraily Daniel O 19, 21, 72
Frazier's Run O 73
Frazier, James 170
Fraizer, Patrich 32
Fram, Francis 187
Frame, David 9, 40, 105, 107, 148, 187
Frame, Margaret 244
Frame, Mathew 87

138 ABSTRACT OF SURVEYS

Frame, Thomas 269
Frame, William 10. 198
Frances, Roderick 246
Francis, John 9. 126, 227
Francisco, Christopher 181
Francisco, Ludwick 23; O 2
Franklin, Edward O 28
Frazee, Ephriam 260, 261
Frazer, David 200
Frazer, Robert 1, 20
Frazur, John O 1, 4, 15
Fridley, Frederick O 76. 82
Fridley, George O 42, 76
Fridley, Lewis 141
Friend, Jacob 163; O 19
Friend, Joseph 28. 67
Frowman's Mill 245
Fu'ch, John 41, 168, 213; O 14, 25, 28
Fule, Andrew 194
Fulk, John O 44, 52, 71
Fulner, Lewis O 83
Fulch, Lowdabauh O 25
Fulton, John 111; O 29, 34
Fulton, Widow O 63, 66
Fultz, George 161
Fultz, John 178
Funk's Hill 165
Fussinger, Nicholas O 98

Gabbard, Cutlip 234
Gad, Samuel O 76
Gain, Daniel O 99
Galespy, Alexander 108
Ga'espy, James 64
Gallespy, Hugh 67, 281
Gallespy, Jacob 126
Gallespy, Robert 53, 64, 159
Gallespy, William 63
Gillespy, Jacob 7
Gamble, James 37. 198
Gamble, Joseph 125, 198, 218
Gardner, Alexander 86
Gardner, Francis 244
Gartin, Uriah O 7, 35
Garton, Elijah 119
Garvin, William 79
Gay, Henry 149, 187
Gay, James 217
Gay, John 217
Gay, Robert 240
George, Thomas 56
Getty, Dennes 73
Getty, Denes 20
Gibbs, Sarah 239, 245
Gibson, David 209
Gibson, George 13, 14
Gibson, John 248
Gibson, Samuel 65, 66, 132, 162
Gibson, William 123
Gilbert, Felix 186, 222, 278; O 36, 37, 54, 73

Gilkeson 38
Gill, Edward 14
Gilmore, David O 76
Gilmore, James 130. 149; O 76
Gilmore, John 14, 115
Gilmore, Thomas 181
Givens, George 110
Givens, James 1, 145, 178
Givens, John. 1, 209, 267
Givens, William 104, 177
Glassprenard, Frederick 190
Glaves O 1
G'en, David 38, 127
Goare, Joseph 173, 174; O 86, 93
Godfrey, Christian 108
Good, Conrod 58
Goodenborg, Jasper 228
Gooding, Daniel 67, 107
Goodpasture, Solom 225
Gorden, Authur 263
Gorden, John 103, 117, 118
Gorden, Thomas O 89
Gorden's Run O 76
Gongle, Andrew 235; O 33
Grabil, John O 47, 49
Grags, William 278
Graham, Archibald 72
Graham, Francis 78, 96
Graham, William 16, 20, 68
Graham, Arthur 181
Grass, David 140
Gratton, John 17, 29, 89, 125, 127, 244, 284; O 4, 13, 14, 53
Great Carolina Road O 53
Great Road 27, 115, 127, 140, 149, 151, 165, 176, 189, 200, 246; O 2, 16, 53, 62, 64, 66, 71, 73, 84, 86
Greathouls, Herman 239
Green, Edward 159
Green, Ezekiael 7, 49, 57; O 15, 16, 18, 71
Green Francis 11 184, 186, 190, O 65, 71, 106
Green, Grant 168
Green, Hugh 161, 176, 183
Green James 11, 88
Green, Robert 6
Gregg, Robert 93
Gregg, Thomas 37
Gregg, William 94, 235, 242, 265
Gregory, Mary 271
Gregory, William 200, 277
Grey, Jacob 205
Grey, Robert 159, 188
Grider, Martin O 72, 80, 81, 92
Griffeth Abel 240
Griffins 33, 34, 75
Grohonis, William 84
Gross, Jacob 213
Grove, O 85

Hedrick, John 2, 168, 181, 213
Heggon, William 125
Heins, Edward 115
Helfrey, John O 14, 15, 21, 81, 92
Hemphill, Samuel 37, 38, 141, 142, 278; O 29, 60, 68, 71
Henderson, Daniel 117, 196, 197
Henderson, Daniel 159
Henderson, James 125
Henderson, John 101
Henderson, Robert 120
Henderson, Samuel 39, 101, 178, 195, 209, 267
Henderson, William 195
Hends, Sam 161, 176
Henry, John O 2
Henpenstall, Abraham 219
Henries O 37
Henry, Henry O 76
Henton, William O 14, 15, 97
Heplinger, Adam O 54
Herdman, John O 84
Herlin, Jacob 261
Hermon, John 50
Herring, William 145, 201; O 5, 35, 94, 95
Herron, Alexander 9, 17, 37, 129
Herron, Leonard O 4, 6
Herseman, Catharine O 26
Herseman, Oldrick 30; O 26
Heston O 85
Hetner, Jacob O 52
Hetvick, Charles O 57, 73
Hewit, Thomas O 29
Hicklin, Thomas 219
Hicks, John O 65
Hilard O 89
Hill 39
Hily, Cornelius 180
Hilyard, Jonathan 180
Hinds, John 90
Hinds, Margaret 234, 236
Hinds, Samuel 8, 234
Hinds, William 234, 236
Hinkle, Isaac O 44
Hinkle, Jacob O 44
Hinkle, Joist 8, 122; O 23
Hinton, John 9, 237
Hinton, Joseph O 37, 76
Hinton, William 151, 152; O 4
Hiron, Samuel 49
Hiser, O 8
Hite, Abraham 6
Hite, Josh 6
Hite, Mines 155
Hite, Phillip O 24, 38, 44
Hoal, Peter 197, 198, 228, 267
Hobby O 70
Hog, James 228
Hog, Peter 233
Hogshead, David 38, 266

Hogshead, James 86, 199
Hogshead, John 185, 241, 266
Hogshead, Michael 38, 94, 241, 266
Holder, Michael O 15, 22
Holman, William 111
Holsinger, Michael O 11, 12
Homes, James 239
Hook, James 226; O 1
Hook, Robert 32; O 1
Hook, Robert, Jr. 32, 208
Hook, William 146, 167; O 1, 25 62
Hopkins, Archibald 28, 118, 279 O 5, 15, 35, 51, 66, 69, 76, 79, 106
Hopkins, John 27; O 6, 29, 83, 84
Hopkins, Thomas O 83, 84
Hopkins, William 279
Hoogler (See Koogler)
Hope O 21
Horn, Christopher O 10
Hornberry, Jacob 165
Hornbrier, Jacob 18
Hover, Bastian 7, 49, 196, 228; O 26, 41
Hover, Michael 211, 225
Howarl, Christopher O 82
Howard, John 136
Howard, Samuel 280
Huffman, George 41; O 14, 25, 62
Huffman, Henry 41
Huffman, Nicholas 1, 41, 168, 213
Hughes, Aaron 9, 102, 155, 237
Hughes, James 19
Hup, John O 62
Huse, O 104
Hudlow, Andrew O 1, 35
Huff's Path 84
Hufft, Jacob O 82, 87, 90, 95
Hugart, James 281
Hugart, William 70
Hughland, Henry 272
Hughland, William 272
Hughland, James 272
Huland, Andrew 241
Hulvey, Conrad O 94
Humble, Conrad O 76
Humble, Martin 86
Humble, Uriah 86
Humphrey, John 148
Humphrey, William 93
Hunter, Samuel 65
Hurrican 82
Hurst, George 192
Huston, Archibald 61, 165; O 17 22, 104
Huston, James 56
Huston, John 147, 205; O 36, 37
Huston, Nathan O 22, 104

ABSTRACT OF SURVEYS        141

Huston, Thomas O 16

Ingle, Thomas 97
Ingle, William 78, 97
Inglish, William 79
Inman, Lazarus 159
Iron, Samuel O 19
Irish, Sink Draft O 32
Irish Path O 86

Jack, Joshua 129
Jackson, John 88, 268; O 100, 101
Jamason, Willaim 68
James, Daniel 153
Jameson, Robert 132, 204
Jarman, Lazarus 171
Jenkins, Joseph 139
Jennings, Branch 241
Jewee, John 45
Joe's Creek O 65
Johnston. Andrew 90, 91, 94, 161
  235; O 7, 30, 46, 64
Johnston, Anthony 59, 269
Johnston, Arthur O 22
Johnston, Hugh 266, 271 282
Johnston, James 258
Johnston, William 87, 178, 195
Jones, Gabriel 42, 55, 70; O 54,
  70, 85
Jones, John 47
Jorden, John 58, 120, 219
Judy, Martin 162, 261
Jump, Mountain 204
Julius, Henry 200

Kaplinger, George 223
Kaplinger, Jacob 155
Kaylor, Frederick 243
Kaylor, Henry 268; O 60
Kaylor, Michael 213; O 28
Keenon, Patrick 159
Keester, Frederick 7, 8
Keez'e, George O 44, 48, 49, 53
  61, 63
Keizer, Martin 53
Kele, George O 6
Keller, Lewis O 40, 93, 94, 104
Kelley, Anthony 110, 204
Kelley, John 115
Kelley, Peter 62, 67
Kelley, Thomas 63
Kelso, Hugh 131, 204, 210, 253
Keneley 201
Kenerly, James 236
Kenerly, Isaac 57
Kenestrick (See Nestrick)
Kennely, Benjamin 7, 17, 88, 103
  116, 119; O 9, 10
Kenney, Bryant 266, 271
Kenney, William 45, 46, 282
Kephart, Henry O 84, 96
Keplinger, Christopher O 85, 101

Keplinger, Henry O 39
Keplinger, John 212, 223; O 81
Keplinger, Phillip 212; O 43
Ketmer. Jacob O 31, 33, 50, 83,
  85, 86
Kerr, James 132, 188, 189, 201,
  234, 271
Kerr, John 7
Kerr, William 234
Kedkley, Francis 44; O 2
Kersh, Mathias 3, 168, 169, 205
  214; O 43
Kertly, Francis 3, 4, 30, 129, 166
  167, 245
Keslinger, Christopher O 25
Keslinger, Henry O 25
Kester, John O 63
Kester, Paul O 66, 75, 76
Kester, Richard O 66, 75
Keys, 202
Kier, (See Kerr)
Kilpatrick, Alexander 184
Kilpatrick, Char'es 184
Kilpatrick, Roger 185
Kimsey, Benjamin 106, 109, 131
King, George 244
King, John 21, 30, 38, 150, 159,
  160, 172, 199, 207, 208. 209, 242
King, Robert 35, 206. 208
King, Thomas O 3, 36
Kingery O 96
Kinkaid, Andrew 122
Kinkaid, John 68, 69, 177
Kinkaid, Samuel 57
Kinkaid, William 57
Kipp, Michael O 31, 65, 85
Kirk, Henry 225
Kirk, John 175
Kirkley, Sinclair O 63
Kirteses Creek O 51
Kiser, Valentine O 61, 62
Kissling, Christopher 3
Kissling, John O 26
Knave (See Neff)
Knox O 75
Knox, Robert 252
Kole, Peter 196
Koogler, George O 92
Koontz, Martin O 63, 91
Koontz, Peter 270
Koontz, Phillip O 92, 96
Kring, John O 18, 19, 95
Kyger, Christian O 14. 70
Kyle, Archebald 22, 137
Kyser, Martin 25

Lachen, Henry 107
Lackey O 38
Laferty, Ralf 177, 220
Lair, Andrew 269
Lair, Joseph O 20
Lair, Mathias 237, 238, 244; O

84
Lair, Widow O 84, 85
Laird, David 226, 237, 238; O 35
43, 59, 67
Laird, James 40, 200; O 44, 60
Lamaston, Richard 259
Lamb, Conrad 17
Lamb, Michael O 81
Lamb, Nicholas 211; O 31
Lamb, William 209, 268; O 13,
51, 62, 80
Lampler 182
Lanahan O 62
Lance, Barnet 197, 266, 268
Lanchan, Dennis O 59
Lancicus, Henry 48, 49, 122
Lang, Charles 155
Lapsley, William 24
Lare, Mathias O 31
Larkins, Henry 68
Lauderdale, James 136
Laufer, John O 14, 21
Lauglin, James 99
Lauglin, John 99
Laurence, James 47, 51, 52, 113
Laurence, Samuel 78, 110, 158
Laurence, Wil'iam 50, 158
Lawrence, Jasem 16, O 53
Layer, James 185
Leaburn, John 93
Leaburn, Henry 118
Leache O 81
Leard, David 116
Leaher, Mathias 28, 40, 119, 201
Leeper, Gawn 125
Leeper, James 207
Leet, Daniel 245
Lehan, Mathias 209
Lemon, John 260
Lemon, Joseph 268
Lewis, Andrew 4, 5, 16, 29, 43,
54, 55, 60, 61, 70, 81, 101, 277
280
Lewis, Anthony O 49, 70
Lewis, Charles 61, 69, 285
Lewis, Colonel 79
Lewis, George 89, 206, 207, 223
Lewis, John 16, 142, 282
Levr's Thomas 16, 23, 29, 42, 67
170, 177; O 37, 70, 77, 81
Lewis, William 22, 23, 81, 206,
244, 267, 271, 282
Lewis, Christopher 190
Lilley, John 237
Lincoln, Abraham O 17, 19
Lincoln, Jacob O 17, 18, 19
Lindon, Joseph 186
Lindsey, Samuel 26
Liner, Henry 146, 216
Lingle, Jacob 102, 226; O 103
Lingle, John 168, 213
Lingle, Lewis O 24

Lingle, Phi'lip 170
Lisk, John 16
Lisk, Samuel 16
Liver, Francis 75
Lochridge, William 240
Lockey, James O 61
Lockey, Thomas O 61
Logan, Benjamin 121, 162
Logan, James 14, 26, 46, 62, 115
212
Logan, John 201
Logue, Samuel 130
Long, Alexander 132, 158, 171,
187, 189
Long (Lung), Henry 2, 41, 200;
O 40
Long, John 149
Long, Joseph 66, 132
Long, William 158, 187, 189
Lookey, Thomas 27, 143, 153,
174, 270; O 16, 18, 61, 76, 81,
86, 92
Looney, John 15, 72, 137
Looney, Joseph 135
Looney, Mary 137
Looney, Peter 135
Looney, Robert 14, 134
Lore (Lohr), Mathias O 31
Lough, Adam 202, 236; O 57
Lough, George O 57
Love, Daniel 18, 38, 143, 163;
O 13, 20, 71
Love, Ephriam 27; O 20
Low, John 13, 24, 67
Lowdabauh, Joseph O 25, 28
Lowdaback, David 178
Lowe, Christopher 49
Lowery, Conrad O 58
Lowery, John 53
Lowery, James 212
Lowry, Patrick 158
Lowthee, Robert 56
Lucas, George 25
Lush O4
Lusk, Hugh 24
Lush, John 181
Lyle, John 204, 253
Lynch, Barnet 60, 157
Lytle, David 108

McAfee, James 22, 47
McAnair, Robert 133
McAnelly, John 56
McBride, Francis 210
McBride, Wil'iam 108, 148
McCah, William 52
McCalester, James 62
McCalister, Eligah O 35
McCamey, William 185
McCarney, 19
McCaumis O 3, 8

McCaury, Hugh 189
McCellon 124
McClanahan, Alexander 56
McClanahan, William 48, 49, 51
McCleery, James 163
McC'eery, Samuel 163
McClellon, John 77, 138
McClellon, William 77, 96
McClenahan, John 229, 230, 231
  232
McClenahan, Robert 36, 51, 89,
  116
McClune, Arthur 15
McClune, Halbart 13, 62, 133
McClune, Samuel 36, 111
McClung, James 36, 108, 203
McC'ung, John 269,
McClung, Samuel 269
McClure, Andrew 175, 178, 201
McClure, Arthur 36, 114, 160
McClure, John 25, 53, 201
McClure, Moses 130
McClure, Nathaniel 112
McClure, Samuel 26, 36, 68
McClure, William 202
McCockey. Peter 246
McColm, Patrick 68
McComb, Andrew 37, 208, 209
McCome, David O 3
McConnel, Patrick 111, 148, 149
McCorcle, A'exander 26, 68
McCord, David 133
McCorner 51
McCown 75
McCoy, James 19, 282
McCoy, John 19, 200, 183
McCoy, William 283
McCrasken, Samuel 113
McCreery. John 148
McCulough, John 42
McCutchin, Robert 40, 120, 195,
  207, 242
McCutchin, William 9, 101
McCutchin, William 105
McDonald, Joseph 78
McDonnel O 99
McDowell, James 15, 69; O 37, 52
McElahaney, William 130
McFar'in. Alexander O 18, 86
McFeters, Samuel 87, 118, 119
McGavick 51
McGavock 133
McGavock, William 203
McGee, Richard 50
McGee, Robert 78
McGlammery, Mathias 172; O
  19, 23
McGlaughlin, Margaret 121
McGill, James O 5, 20
McGill, John 201; O 5
McGill, William 162; O 13, 92
McKay, Robert 6, 129

McKee, John 158
McKee, Samuel 208
McKee, William 132
McKenney, Alexander 164
McKenney, John 164
McKenney, William 114, 266
McKetrick, Robert 175, 184, 185
  198, 265, 266
McKinley O 35
McKinzey 107
McMahan, John 208, 244, 269
McMahon, Thomas 186
McMillin, James 73, 84, 140
McMullan, Edward 79, 80 279
McMullan, William 72, 90
McMunay, William 31, 130. 131,
  158
McMurbry, Joseph 96
McMurray, Samuel 69
McMustray, Joseph 77
McNare, Daniel 241
McNeare, Daniel 58
McNeel, Daniel 135
McNeel, John 74, 85
McNeel. Neal 79
McNeely 245
McNicer O 20
McNiel, William 37
McOnails, Daniel 244
McRoberts, Samuel 76, 77
McVea. John 87. 182; O 3
Mace, Henry O 88
Mace. Nicholas 184
Madison, John 23, 24. 32, 35, 42,
  56. 72, 75, 140, 162
Madison. John Jr. 199, 249
Magee, David 74, 95
Magee, John 139
Magee, Wil'iam 74, 95
Makall, John O 77, 81, 88
Maggot, David O 90
Maggot, Hance (John) 169; O 2
Maggot, Jacob O 90
Maggot, Henry O 90
Malcom, John O 3. 39, 40
Mallow, George 141; O 2
Mal'ow, Michael 127, 157, 196
Manis, Denes 188
Mann, Barnet 2, 43
Mann, Charles 212
Mann, George 43; O 40, 46
Mann, Jacob 2, 43, 168, 213
Mann, Thomas 85, 100
Mann, William 38, 283
Marche (See Martz)
Mare, Hugh 15
Marra, Henry 184
Morra, Samuel 184, 185, 265
Marrow, Daniel O 40
Marshall, Gilbert 97
Marshall, James 94
Marshel O 75

144        ABSTRACT OF SURVEYS

Marton, John 100
Marton, William 108, 115
Martin, Charles 255
Martin, George 146
Martz, Boston O 18, 72, 90, 92
Mathew, Barnaba 103, 107, 123
Mathew, David 194, 265
Mathew, George 19, 69, 176
Mathew, John 45
Mathew, Lasley O 44
Mathew, Richard O 21, 22
Mathew, Robert O 6. 21
Mathew. Sampson 19, 56, 69.
    176, 244
Mathew, Solomon O 20. 21, 30.
    65, 69, 81, 83. 87, 102
Mathew, Townsend 151, 157; O
    9, 10, 21
Mathew, William 265, 271
Mathus, William 175
Maurice, John 260. 261
Maurice, Richard 262. 263
Maxwell, James 41, 159
Means, Hugh 189
Mealows, Francis 166; O 90
Meek, John 112
Me'lecan. Moses 85, 95
Mel'on, James 140
Mellon. John 74
Merrow, James 27, 149
Mesick, Elihu O 66, 77
Metscaw, Valentine 161
Michael, Frederick O 51
Michael, William O 40 46
Miller, Abraham 141, 169; O 32,
    38, 66, 84
Miller, Alexander 121, 143, 163.
    190, 227, 237. 238; O 13, 22, 59
Mil'er, Andrew 77
Mi'ler. Ann 112
Miller, Braham O 65
Miller, Casner 119
Mi'ler, Christian 169
Miller, David O 37. 82
Miller, Henry 43, 169, 240; O 6,
    8. 9, 36, 96
Miller, Hugh 105
Mil'er, Isaac O 64, 65, 84
Miller, Jacob 30
Miller, James 107
Miller, John 77. 86, 94, 105, 205,
    212; O 65, 68, 78
Miller, Leonard 238, B244; O 17
    22, 78, 93. 94, 104
Miller, Patrick 187
Miller, Peter 2, 40, 200; O 2, 43
Miller, Robert 25
Mil'er, Samuel O 22, 64, 65, 71
Miller, Stephen O 79
Miller, Thomas 2, 121
Miller, Widow O 84
Miller, William 77

Mills, Amos 264
Mills, Hugh 35, 84, 136
Mil's, John 72, 135, 136, 137
Millsap 154
Minnick, John O 6. 31, 66, 86
Minnis, Robert O 34, 79
Minter, William 195
Mire, Jacob 4
Mitchcar, Nicholas 236
Mitchell, David 97, 135
Mitchell, James 106, 131, 204
Mitchell, John 50
Mizell, Jacob 223, 224
Moal, Edward 209
Moats, Jacob 193
Moffett, George 126, 241, 243, 244
Moffett, James 39, 204
Moffett, John 126
Monger, John 167, 168; O 63
Monger, Wil'iam 43, 222
Moniee, James 179
Monsey, Francis 27
Montgomery, James 38, 53, 76
Montgomery, John 45
Moore. James 51, 73
Moore, John 100. 155, 158; O 37
Moore, Samuel 68, 69
Moore, Thomas 28, 143, 153, 176,
    237, 262, 270ffi O 16, 72, 90
Moore, William 76
Moon, Moses 283
Morgan, Charles 229
Moris, Richard 38
Morris O 76
Morris, Daniel 124
Morris, John O 45
Moser, Adam 235
Moses, Jacob O 61
Mossey (Mauzy), Elihu 268
Mouldrough, Jean 68, 69
Mount, George 156
Mouse 39
Moyer, Michael 224; O 15
Moyers, Jacob O 61, 67
Moze, Joseph 37
Mullen, Michael 96; O 13, 60, 80
Mullin, Mathey, 31
Munay, James O 5, 83
Muncey, Bryan 119
Murphee, Hugh 161, 236
Murphy, Laurence 282
Murrie or Murry O 35. 76, 91, 96
Myas, William 107, 187

Nacob, Christopher 217
Naked Creek (Shenandoah, Dan-
    iel Sink) 3
Naked Creek Burktown, (John
    Carpenter) 16
Nall, William O 68
Nalls, 11
Naper, William 45

Needham, John 152, 172, 178; O 21, 97
Neegley, George 226, 242
Neely, James 21, 33, 54, 71, 84
Neely, John 21, 50, 62
Neely, Robert 72
Neff, Henry 39, 40; O 29, 32, 87
Neigley, Christian 197
Neighley, Paulser 125
Neil, Charles 165
Nelson, Daniel O 17, 20, 21, 51 59
Nelson, John 194; O 45
Nelson, Thomas 56
Nestricks, John O 24, 38, 65, 66
Nichols, Andrew 244
Nichols, Robert 244
Nicholas, George 198
Nicholas, Jacob 47, 141, 181
Nicholas, John 87, 88
Nicholas, Michael O 56
Nicholas, Samuel 88, 225
Nivil, John 250
Noble, John 108
No'e, William O 2
Norton, O 30
Nox, James 282
Nox, Robert 282
Null, George 3; O 67
Null, Henry 4, 86; O 67
Null, Nicholas 3, 44; O 63

Oback, Adam O 31, 63
Obryan, James 14
Ofrail, Moris 14, 130, 176
Ohler, (See Eiler)
Ogan, Thomas O 88
Oldham, William 207, 227
Oliboust, Michael 59
Oliver, John O 4, 6
Onval, John 221
Owe, Christopher 228

Pace (See Poss)
Packett, Dursy 96
Pickett, Drusy 99
Painter, Alexander 155
Painter, Leonard O 17, 91
Panninger, Henry 18, 37, 49, 155 228
Pap, John Christman O 32
Passinger, Jacob 158
Parker, James 265
Parks, John 202
Parson, James 260
Parson, Thomas 57, 236, 259
Passinger (See Persinger)
Paterson O 21
Patterson, James 37, 128, 209, 214
Patterson, John 44, 84, 138, 206, 207, 209

Patterson, Joseph 227
Patterson, Margaret 16, 163
Patterseon, Robert 117, 186, 269
Patterson, William 19, 102
Patton, Mathew 209, 265; O 27, 48
Paul, Audly 46, 158
Paulson, Benjamin 73, 84
Paxton, John 15, 111
Paxton, Samuel 45
Paxton, Thomas 31
Pearcey, O 39
Pearisioner, Jacob 119, 120
Peartree, John 174
Peck, Jacob 244
Pence, Adam O 14
Pence, George O 14, 59
Pence, Henry O 85
Pence, Jacob 145
Pence, John O 85
Pence, William O 25, 39
Peopler, Lewis O 71
Perigan, William 270
Perkey, Ann 2
Perkey, Jacob O 84, 85
Perkey, John 167; O 14
Perkey, Henry 1, 2, 167; O 1, 25
Perrine, Henry O 56
Perry, James 131
Persinger, Jacob 2, 97, 181; O 2
Peterfish, Conrod 86; O 2, 25, 26, 84
Peters, Jacob 9, 18, 165, 192, 213 O 2, 38
Peters, John O 2
Peterscern, John 225
Peterson, Michael 48
Peterson, William O 79
Petijohn, William O 33, 47, 65
Petner, John O 66, 82, 87
Pharis, Edward 105
Pharis, John O 56
Phifer, Adam O 12, 31, 37, 65
Phillips, Evin O 35
Phillips, James 27, 163, 175
Phillips, John 28, 56, 153, 163, 176, 241, 271; O 16, 35
Phips, John 88, 210
Pickett, Thomas 142
Pickerns, William O 27, 64
Pickering, William 86
Pickins, Thomas 125
Pickle, Henry 194
Pickle, Jacob 49, 57
Pitman, John O 65
Poage, George 9
Poage, John 30, 56, 68, 78, 93, 111, 115, 125, 157, 161, 176, 184, 196, 198, 206, 208 244 267
Poage, Robert 100
Poage, Thomas 206
Poage, William 45

Summers, John 107, 133, 147
Summerville, Thomas 194
Summerfield, Joseph O 33
Swadley, Henry 234; O 27, 41
Swadley, Mark 8, 196; O 41
Swords Land 39
Sweet, Timothy 123
Swing, Godfrey O 49, 61, 85
Switzer, Henry 11, 224
Switzer's Meadow 3
Symmon, Laurence 126
Sympson, James 114, 160
Sympson, John 131

Talman, Benjamin O 72
Talman, William O 72
Tanner, John 244; O 17, 40, 70
Tanner, Michael O 22, 40
Tany, William 99
Tarbut, Hugh 203
Tate, David 63
Tate, John 114
Taylor, David 220; O 60
Taylor, George 24, 52, 252
Taylor, Isaac 80
Taylor, John 65, 147, 165; O 15
  35, 44, 45, 46, 85
Teas, Charles 143, 145
Teas, William 171
Teeter, Christian 179, 205
Teeter, George 123; O 46
Teeter, Paul 124, 168, 235
Teeter, Phillip 191
Templeton, James 111
Terrel, Peter O 33
Terry, William 74
Thom, Michael 56
Thom, Tobias 56
Thomas, Evon 88, 190
Thomas, James 11, 88, 168
Thomas, John 88, 182, 211; O 32
  102
Thomas, Joseph 155
Thomas, Reese 182, 184; O 51
Thompson, Edward 220
Thompson, James 24
Thompson, John 75, 97, 181
Thompson, Mathew 30, 32, 146,
  226; O 1
Thompson, Samuel 54
Thompson, William 70, 97, 131,
  220
Thompson, Moses 121, 193, 199
Thornhill, Samuel 4, 168, 205
Tickout, Balser O 45
Ticktum, Richard 94
Tilford, James 31, 214, 216
Toebly, George David O 45
Tolmans O 75
Tootwiler, Leonard O 14, 22, 40
Tosh, Thomas 21, 34, 76, 85
Tresler, Peter 168; O 26

Timble, David 25
Trimble, James 24, 31, 36, 62, 66
  68, 69, 108, 112, 130, 133, 156
  185
Trimble, John 253
Trimble, Moses 160
Trimble, Walter 51, 103
Tross, Jacob 268
Trotter, James 89, 125
Trotter, John 17, 129
Trout, George 44, 145, 146
Trumbo, Jacob O 50, 71, 80, 85
Turk, Thomas 143, 201, 234; O
  70
Turpine, Solomon 28, 40, 151; O
  100
Try River in Brock's Gap O 82

Vance, John 271
Vance, Samuel 202, 268
Vance, William O 72
Vanderpool's Gap 13, 148
Vandevender, Jacob O 78
Van Farson, Joachim 170; O 48
  61, 85, 87, 88
Vanpelt, Peter O 66
Vanpelt, Tunis O 12, 66
Vansent, Isiah 139
Vatter, William O 28
Venimon, Peter 58, 122, 195, 198
  O 16, 55, 58
Verden, Edaniah 37
Vineyard, Christopher 132
Vise (See Wise)

Wade, Dawson 108, 238
Waddle, Thomas 182
Waggy, Phillip O 29
Waggoner, Christian 196
Waggoner, Christopher 27, 207,
  266
Waggoner, Lewdwick 18, 209;
  O 26
Waldrum, George 192
Walker, Alexander 14, 89, 113,
  132, 164, 175, 177, 186, 204,
  208
Walker Benjamin 123
Walker, James 229, 230, 253
Walker, John 14, 51, 113, 115,
  132
Walker, Samuel 36, 46, 105, 130
Walker, Thomas 101
Wallace, David 52, 132
Wallace, John 66
Wallace, Peter 111
Wallace, Robert 103
Waller, Henry 114
Warmley, John 91
Ward, James 63
Ware, John O 43, 49, 59
Warrel, Samuel 262